Compañeros

Compañeros

Two Communities in a Transnational Communion

∽

JOE GATLIN, NANCY GATLIN,
AND JOEL H. SCOTT

WIPF & STOCK · Eugene, Oregon

COMPAÑEROS
Two Communities in a Transnational Communion

Copyright © 2017 Joe Gatlin, Nancy Gatlin, and Joel H. Scott. All rights reserved. Except for brief quotations in critical publications or reviews, no part of this book may be reproduced in any manner without prior written permission from the publisher. Write: Permissions, Wipf and Stock Publishers, 199 W. 8th Ave., Suite 3, Eugene, OR 97401.

Wipf & Stock
An Imprint of Wipf and Stock Publishers
199 W. 8th Ave., Suite 3
Eugene, OR 97401

www.wipfandstock.com

PAPERBACK ISBN: 978-1-5326-1981-6
HARDCOVER ISBN: 978-1-5326-1983-0
EBOOK ISBN: 978-1-5326-1982-3

Manufactured in the U.S.A.   DECEMBER 1, 2017

"Vamos Todos al Banquete" by Guillermo Cuéllar
Copyright © 1988, GIA Publications, Inc.
All rights reserved. Used by permission.

Photo Credits
Introduction—Dawn Noelle Smith Beutler
Chapter 1—Joe Gatlin
Chapter 2—David Janzen
Chapter 3—Joe Gatlin
Chapter 4—Joe Gatlin
Chapter 5—Joe Gatlin
Chapter 6—Dawn Noelle Smith Beutler
Chapter 7—Dawn Noelle Smith Beutler
Chapter 8—Joe Gatlin
Chapter 9—Rodrigo Godoy

To the memory of Jorge Molina,
A friend and facilitator of our transnational communion,
and Executive Director of Habitat for Humanity El Salvador
for eighteen years

Contents

Preface | ix

    Introduction: Two Communities, the Chasm, Communion, and the Table of Creation | 1

Section 1: The Great Chasm

    Chapter 1   The Witness of Romero | 21
    Chapter 2   Beginning a Friendship | 31

Section 2: Practices of a Transnational Communion

    Chapter 3   Suffering | 45
    Chapter 4   Giving Thanks | 55
    Chapter 5   Sharing | 65
    Chapter 6   Remembering | 81
    Chapter 7   Proclaiming | 97

Section 3: The Table of Creation

    Chapter 8   Lessons Learned | 113
    Chapter 9   Looking Forward: Our Call to Action | 129

Discussion Guide for Those from the North | 139
Bibliography | 143

Preface

WE WERE SEVERAL YEARS into writing this book before we discovered what we were doing.

At first we thought we were helping a community of Salvadoran *campesinos* (fieldworkers) capture their history in written form. Their breath-taking and tragic account of fleeing their country with government death squads literally on their heels needs to be told and preserved in circles much larger than just those of their small community in El Salvador known as Valle Nuevo of Santa Marta. Their stories include generations of subjugation on the *estancias* (ranches) of the northern department of Cabañas, a night-time flight along rocky, mountain paths in 1981, the massacre at the Lempa River as they tried to reach safety in Honduras, their growth in solidarity despite destitution and disease through eight years in United Nations sponsored refugee camps in Honduras, and the return to their homeland in 1989 as a disenfranchised yet determined people.

It is a remarkable saga, and the elders of their community tell it with pathos and conviction. Their accounts are replete with vivid images of a bullet-ridden chair, a shrapnel garden, a pillar of light that led them in the night, a base community reading Scripture in a hidden cave, a teacher with only a second-grade education, a champion high-school swimmer who magically appeared when they were trying to cross the swollen river, and Christ hanging on the cross of free trade. Since their repatriation, they have built a community in the Salvadoran countryside and persevered through hunger, depression, death, mental illness, discrimination, alcoholism, illiteracy, the destruction of their farm-based economy by free trade laws, and the exploitation of their land by foreign corporations.

Preface

Our progress on the manuscript, however, was slow. Every year we found ourselves backing up and starting over as we tried to capture new concepts and insights discovered through our visits, phone calls, and adventures. With the passage of time—as we moved past the twenty-year anniversary of Shalom Mission Communities' first visit to Valle Nuevo—our relationship deepened and matured and our perspective changed, and we could not escape the feeling that we were missing something in our writing.

About four years ago, as the three of us sat in a Waco coffee shop musing over the reasons for our fits and starts, the realization hit us that the story we needed to tell was not just their story, but our story, the story of two communities, one in El Salvador and one in the United States, building a relationship. There was immediate clarity; writing about our relationship was what we should be doing. Several developments supported this new direction.

One, the elders of Valle Nuevo had become less desperate in sharing their experience of suffering and loss. Maybe the turning point had come after the hundredth re-telling. It seemed they had relaxed and begun, albeit slowly, the process of healing from the trauma. Their offspring had embraced their history and made it their own. Their friends from the north were not going away; year after year they were returning and still listening. And there was a locally organized effort underway to capture and preserve their oral history.

A second reason for shifting the focus was that those of us from the United States were better able to articulate what this relationship meant to us. We realized the story we told about our friendship with the Salvadorans was about our own transformation. We were not in this relationship to record a deed of mercy or to set right a wrong, but instead to find forgiveness, wholeness, and redemption for ourselves.

A third reason, we had found it is just not easy to describe this experience to others. Those of us from the north are asked, "Why are you going to El Salvador again? Whose pictures are these on your wall?" Standard categories of north-south encounters are short-term mission or exposure trips with relief, development, or study as an objective, but none of these apply. We struggle to find a way with just a few words to explain our relationship and justify the effort and expense we invest in it.

Conversely, our friends from Valle Nuevo also have told us of their difficulties. They are often asked, "Who are these *gringos* that keep showing up? Why are they so special to you?" Their answer that they are friends and

PREFACE

practically family is met with quizzical looks and outright skepticism. So, with stories and reflections, we attempt in *Compañeros* to paint a picture that can better explain this relationship we've come to call our transnational communion.

While we do commend this type of relationship to others, we are quick to say we have not created a how-to-manual for other communities south or north. It was never our intention to do so. There are no checklists, no sequenced steps, no articulated theory of change, no benchmarks, no measures of success provided herein. For those who are interested we have just these few pieces of advice: 1) resist evil's power to draw boundaries, create borders, and dig chasms in this world; 2) listen to the Holy Spirit; 3) "work out your own salvation with fear and trembling" (Phil 2:12).

And we offer a blessing and hope, Christ prepares a table where language, culture, and national politics no longer have the power to divide.

HOW THIS BOOK WAS WRITTEN

Through the decades many individuals from Shalom Mission Communities have written and shared journal entries and articles about their trips to Valle Nuevo and reflections about the rare occasions when *campesinos* have been able to visit the Shalom communities stateside. Most of these pieces have appeared in "Shalom Connections," our associational newsletter that is available on the Shalom Mission Communities website. In keeping with the Shalom Mission ethos, we have treated these intellectual perspectives and spiritual insights as communal property. Direct quotes and excerpts are credited within. Special acknowledgement is given to Dawn Noelle Smith Beutler of Church of the Sojourners and David Janzen of Reba Place Fellowship for contributions to the text of the book.

Because the *campesinos* of Valle Nuevo have more of an oral than a written tradition, we have recorded about seventeen hours of their stories and remembrances of the community's history and its relationship with Shalom Mission Communities. We have also captured a number of quotes from various conversations and meetings in the last several years. In addition, some of the university-educated young adults from the community have written reflections that appear in this book.

The concept of the book has been developed through many discussions during Shalom Mission associational meetings and conversations on the verandahs of Valle Nuevo homes. The last several years we regularly

Preface

have a designated time for "theological reflection" with the *directiva* (the governing board of elders) during our Valle Nuevo visits. There we simply read one of Jesus's parables, a narrative, or another verse of Scripture and then ask, "Who are we in this story?" or "We've been struggling with this Scripture back at home, trying to understand what it means for us; what do you think?" An hour or two of discussion always follows with rich insights of how the Scripture reads in our respective contexts as well as our relationship. These sessions have given shape to the ideas and metaphors in this book.

Once a draft of each chapter was finished, we would translate it and send it to Valle Nuevo for their input and review. Reminiscent of how epistles were shared in the first century church, a large circle of people would gather on one of their verandahs and listen to the current installment as it was read out loud. At every step along the way we have stopped to listen to the feedback so we could make sure we faithfully and honestly are capturing the spirit and details of our common story.

THE IMPORTANCE OF WORDS

As explained herein, the Spanish word '*compañeros*' carries more relational substance than its English counterpart, 'companion', and thus our choice of title. Our friends in Valle Nuevo are sensitive to the gender-exclusivity of this word, so the Spanish edition is titled accordingly *Compañeros y Compañeras*.

From this point forward we will no longer use the word 'we' to refer to the authors of this book or to those of us from the United States. This is a communal effort to explain a communion of communities; there is no further place in this account for a "we" and a "they." The first-person plural will be used for the collective voice of both Valle Nuevo and Shalom Mission. The reader will need to discern the "we" in quotes or reflections of specific individuals.

The next section will introduce the community of Valle Nuevo and its relationship with the larger village of Santa Marta. "Valle Nuevo," "Valle Nuevo of Santa Marta," "Santa Marta," "the *campesinos*," and occasionally "the Salvadorans" will all generally refer to the same community.

Shalom Mission Communities is the name of a small association of Christian communities in the United States. The next section will introduce the individual groups. The association is referred to as "Shalom Mission

Communities," "Shalom Mission," or "SMC." "The Shalom Mission communities" (lower-case 'c') is used in reference to the identities, activities, or actions of the individual communities.

One additional matter of style, because Central America is part of North America, we do not use "North American" to distinguish the people of the United States from the people of El Salvador.

Scripture quotations are from the New Revised Standard Version of the Bible unless otherwise indicated.

At the midpoint of the span over the great chasm where our two peoples have met, we are encountering God's grace, forgiveness, and wholeness. Although the void below us is still plainly visible, we have been given hope that the chasm will one day be filled.

On behalf of the contributing members of Valle Nuevo and the communities of Shalom Mission, it is our prayer that this book will stir hearts including our own toward a more holistic, inclusive examination of our humanity and the Spirit's work in the world.

Shalom—

Joe Gatlin, Nancy Gatlin, & Joel H. Scott
Members of Hope Fellowship, a member of Shalom Mission Communities

Introduction

Two Communities, the Chasm, Communion, and the Table of Creation

THE CHASM

Between you and us a great chasm has been fixed,
so that those who might want to pass from here to you cannot do so,
and no one can cross from there to us.

(Luke 16:26)

COMMUNION

For as often as you eat this bread and drink the cup,
you proclaim the Lord's death until he comes.

(1 Corinthians 11:26)

THE TABLE OF CREATION

Let's go now to the banquet,
To the table of creation,
Where each one with their own chair
Has a place and a mission to share.

(Translated from the Misa Popular—
"Vamos Todos al Banquete")

Introduction

Margarita Avilez, Juana Lainez, and Carol Youngquist rest on the way to the Lempa

TWO COMMUNITIES

ON A THURSDAY MORNING in late June we always go down to the river. A couple dozen of us, half from Valle Nuevo and half from the United States, squeeze into Carlos's two micro-buses for a bumpy ride along the rocky, red-dirt road that hugs mountainsides, dips in and out of ravines, and passes isolated *campesino* houses. We eventually cross one final stream and then pull left onto a rocky bank where everyone piles out, stretching to reboot bodies that have turned numb.

A few head off to find bushes suitable for bathroom needs while the rest fill water bottles and chat and wait. Salomé Ascencio, with his machete, cuts walking sticks for the elders to help them keep their footing on the steep and rocky path. There is no hurry and no impatience because togetherness is the primary goal of this outing as well as the entire, week-long Shalom Mission Communities delegation to Valle Nuevo. When all are back together we cross the road and skinny between two posts that create a narrow v-gate in the barbed-wire. Then it is down the footpath, through the cow pasture, under or over a couple of fences more. We will stop to rest at the halfway point while we maneuver everyone over a four-foot high stone fence.

From there we get our first view of the river as it makes a sweeping bend through the surrounding hills. It is beautiful and peaceful; the line that is drawn down the middle of it to separate El Salvador from Honduras is imperceptible. It is difficult for those from the states to imagine that day when it was a chasm of terror and death, but for the *campesinos* who were there on a Thursday morning in March, 1981, the sight of the Lempa stirs a very deep sadness. One or more may hum a mournful song, and, if she is with us, Juana Lainez will lead out in a softly sung ballad about their journey through the chasm.

When we finally are sitting with our feet in the river, stories are inevitably shared as the people of Valle Nuevo identify rocks where they attempted to hide from bullets, a particular spot or two or three where loved ones—mortally wounded—fell, the place on the bank where they managed to tie a rope and stretch it across the river, or the bend further down where they last saw a mother flailing her arms, trying to reach a child as they both were washed away.

VALLE NUEVO

The chasm was fixed in the Lempa River valley that March 18. The stories will never be forgotten because they are now told by many, not just those who made it safely across the river, but also by their children, their grandchildren, and their friends from Shalom Mission Communities. Even though it was almost a decade later that the *campesinos* took the name Valle Nuevo, the community was born on that awful day. Out of tragedy and death a people came into being, a people who through suffering and survival found solidarity and community.

A couple of years earlier, after generations of festering discontent over the lack of land tenure, employment, wages, and political rights, civil war had erupted in El Salvador. On March 17, 1981, word traveled from village to village in the northern department of Cabañas that government-sponsored death squads were advancing through the district, scorching the earth, and slaughtering the people. That evening the *campesinos* fled their homes and took to the mountain paths under the cover of dark. It was a night of panic and chaos as thousands of people tried to escape and find their way to Honduras where they hoped they would be safe. Men, women, and youth tripped over roots and rocks as they carried babies and guided children and the elderly. Hunger, thirst, and exhaustion built through the night.

The *campesinos* had lived as peasants for generations, abjectly working the fields and serving as slaves of the landowners. In recent years, some of them had found hope and dignity as well as a voice when they read the words of Jesus, "He has sent me to proclaim release to the captives and recovery of sight to the blind, to let the oppressed go free" (Luke 4:18), and heard in their souls the song of Mary, "He has filled the hungry with good things, and sent the rich away empty" (Luke 1:53). Disregarding the canonical status and divine inspiration of these passages, the landowners declared these sentiments subversive and responded with threats of violence. The people, however, continued to meet in small groups known as base communities in caves and other hidden places where they could safely read their Bibles and reflect on the relevance of the gospel to their world.

Some, in their determination to put food on the table and provide for their families, took up arms and joined guerrilla forces in an effort to bring down the government. The military, though, with contributions from United States taxpayers, was well-armed, well-equipped, and therefore capable of squashing any perceived conspiracy or actual insurgency. As the turmoil in the country increased, the authorities declared that extermination of the *campesinos* was the only solution in some rural areas where the infestation of guerrillas and guerrilla-supporters was so severe.

The *campesinos* stumbled down from the mountains that Thursday morning with the death squads, burning fields, forests, and homes, in hot pursuit. Some four thousand men, women, and children, young and old, arrived at the banks of the Lempa where their terror was compounded when helicopters hovered low and rained gunfire upon them. Bullets pierced flesh and caromed off rocks while many, bleeding and dying, cringed under boulders. Escape back into the hills was cut off. It seemed that gunfire was coming not just from El Salvador but also from the other side of the river, making them wonder if the Honduran military had not been recruited to the mission of their annihilation. The river's current that day appeared to be especially swift and the water deeper than usual; years later the *campesinos* would suspect the government purposefully had made the crossing deadlier by opening a dam upstream.

Up in the Honduran hills Yvonne Dilling, a young Church of the Brethren volunteer from Fort Wayne, Indiana, was bandaging the wounds

Two Communities, The Chasm, Communion...

of recently arrived Salvadoran refugees. In Yvonne's account the flow of refugees stopped about three in the afternoon.

> I asked those who were still resting under the tree whether more people would be coming, and they answered, "Oh, there are hundreds! Hundreds and hundreds!" But they weren't arriving.... I asked, "What is taking them so long to get up here?" A man responded, "Well, they need to cross a deep river, and the few swimmers who can carry them across are exhausted. They, too, have been without food for three days...."[1]

Yvonne said she could not bear the frustration of "watching helicopters fly around and listening to bombs fall," so she went down to the river where she discovered there were only five swimmers among the desperate thousands present. She became the sixth, and as a result many more *campesinos* were able to cross to safety.

The Lempa survivors would live for the next eight years as exiles in refugee camps where many continued to die from starvation and disease. They were exiles long enough for children to be born and know nothing other than refugee life and long enough for some of the elders to pass on. Life was hard, but the people banded together to govern themselves, to teach and educate their children, and to take care of the elderly and sick.

By 1989, a number of Salvadoran war refugees began to repatriate. In October of that year a group, with the blessing and support of the United Nations, left the Mesa Grande camp in Honduras, crossed into El Salvador, and traveled to the outskirts of Santa Marta, a village in Cabañas where two previous groups of returnees had already settled. They were directed to a neighborhood called Valle Nuevo. In their first weeks, they constructed houses with salvaged lumber chinked with mud and planted fields on the rocky sides of the surrounding mountains. They also created their own governing board, or *directiva*, and turned to the work of building a new economy and social institutions in the middle of the Salvadoran jungle.

The *campesinos*, who had been exploited as serfs by the landowners, labeled as seditious by their government, and hunted and murdered by the death squads, returned from Honduras with no money, no land, and no material possessions other than a few personal items and scavenged building materials from the refugee camp. The "peace" of the Chapultepec Peace Accords in 1992 would mean only the cessation of armed conflict for the people of Valle Nuevo. The agreement did not bring that more profound

1. Dilling, *In Search*, 42–43.

Introduction

sense of peace that is captured in the Hebrew word of *shalom*, a state of harmony, sufficiency, and well-being.

They also returned with no social status. The nearby community of Victoria, the seat of the *municipalidad* (a smaller division of governing units within El Salvador), had long been a stronghold of ARENA (Alianza Republicana Nacionalista), the traditionally conservative political party within El Salvador that represented the interests of the landowners and the established business community. The people of Santa Marta and Valle Nuevo had been aligned with the guerrilla movement and, therefore, were still deemed rabble and considered a social burden by the governing party. And even within Santa Marta, where they were the last migration to arrive, the *campesinos* of Valle Nuevo felt like outcasts.

Among the inevitable by-products of slavery and war are physical, emotional, and mental illnesses. Discriminated against and disenfranchised, rejected and refugees, scarred and scared, the people of Valle Nuevo were left and ignored outside the gate of acceptability and wealth.

The brothers and sisters of Valle Nuevo are not, however, docile victims. From Honduras, they brought back tremendous spiritual assets: a powerful sense of community built on the foundation of their common suffering and loss, a profound faith grounded in a narrative inspired by liberation theology, and well-developed organizational skills that were a necessity for survival in the refugee camps.

Today Santa Marta has a population of around five thousand people with about one thousand of those living in Valle Nuevo. Over time, with population growth and the aging of children who share one school system serving all of Santa Marta, the difference between Valle Nuevo and Santa Marta has become difficult to discern. The self-identification of "Valle Nuevo" and the maintenance of a *directiva* is important for the elders but less so for the youth, several of whom have returned from university studies in the capital San Salvador to take leadership roles in the community, the school, and in development projects.

SHALOM MISSION COMMUNITIES

In another base community movement, almost five hundred years ago, three young men in a living room in Zurich, Switzerland, studied Scripture and then baptized each other. Shockingly, to all of the church and state officials, none of them were priests. It was the birth of what has been called the radical arm of the Protestant Reformation.

Anabaptists, as they came to be known, grew rapidly in numbers, and because of their refusal to practice infant baptism, whereby the authorities registered and taxed its people, and to take up arms, which the Anabaptists saw as a violation of the command of Christ, they were viewed as subversives by both church and state. They were persecuted, martyred, and driven underground, and like so many Christians through the ages, found themselves meeting in caves, fields, and barns.

In 1957 a group of Mennonite students and voluntary service workers seeking to recover the profound commitment of the early Anabaptists, took up residence together in a large house on Reba Place in south Evanston, Illinois. This intentional Christian community developed a catechism based on the Sermon on the Mount (Matt 5-7) and took to heart the economic practices of the early church in Jerusalem whose members "had all things in common" so that "there was not a needy person among them" (Acts 2:44; 4:34).

Today Reba Place Fellowship is a community of about eighty adults and children living in houses and apartments in one neighborhood and sharing their finances in a common treasury. The fellowship is recognized as the longest-surviving and one of the most influential, urban, Protestant, Christian communities in the United States. It has mentored many Christian communities and given birth to several others including two racially and ethnically diverse, non-communal Mennonite congregations in Evanston and in northeast Chicago.

The members of Reba and the other Shalom Mission communities are also refugees, refugees from a society that is described in their website as relentlessly pursuing "consumption, power, and self." They have also left the mainstream of the various religious traditions—Baptist, Church of Christ, Methodist, Church of God, and other evangelical denominations—from which their members have come. These communities share commitments of service to neighbors, love of enemies, renunciation of personal possessions and material security, and universal ministry of all believers.

Some SMC members might object to—or be embarrassed by—a comparison of their countercultural, faith-based form of communal life to the martyrdom of the early Anabaptists or to the imposed oppression and exploitation of their friends in Valle Nuevo. Nevertheless, SMC and Valle

Introduction

Nuevo feel a common bond in their respective experiences of dislocation within their own societies.

SMC was first formed in 1991 as a partnership of Reba Place and Plow Creek Fellowship, one of Reba's own progeny, located on a farm in Tiskilwa, Illinois. Plow Creek, a community at times of about thirty to forty adults and children, often used its retreat cabin and guest rooms to host urban and international visitors, including one summer some *campesinos* from Valle Nuevo. Over the last decade this community experienced a number of internal struggles and reorganizations, and, after the deaths of three of its elders in early 2017, decided to wind down and disband.

Hope Fellowship began as a communal household of two families in Waco, Texas, in 1994. That same year they traveled one thousand miles north and surprised Reba Place and Plow Creek with a request to join their association. The communities said yes, and SMC began to envision itself as a larger network. Hope Fellowship today is a bilingual (Spanish and English) Mennonite church community of about ninety adults and children living in an inner-city neighborhood. Fellowship members share many possessions, have embraced a commitment that none of their group "will be in need," and are involved in a number of ministries in their neighborhood. Their Anabaptist identity is a contrast to the dominant presence of evangelical Christians in their city.

Church of the Sojourners in San Francisco joined SMC in 1996. Their thirty members and children live with financial-sharing arrangements in three close-by households in the historically-Latino Mission District where they have become a familiar presence in the neighborhood. Their purpose as explained in their website is to "be the church for the world" in their "vibrant, pagan, jam-packed city." Since their founding in 1988, they have carried on an intense community life with regular meetings for discernment, spiritual growth, and Bible study. Several of their group have authored books on Christian discipleship and community.

SMC has developed over time a wider network of communities sometimes called "Shalom Connections." SMC also participates in and supports the Nurturing Communities Project, an effort to bring together older and younger Christian communities in the United States for sharing wisdom, building enthusiasm, and engendering mutual support. One fruit of this inter-generational group is a book by Reba Place member David Janzen, *The Intentional Christian Community Handbook: For Idealists, Hypocrites, and Wannabe Disciples of Jesus*.

Each of the Shalom Mission communities has its own distinct structures and practices for nurturing discipleship through communal life, finances, and worship. Despite the distances that separate them and beyond the other associational and denominational connections they maintain, they have found their inter-communal relationships of support, accountability, and fellowship to be invaluable. Relationships between the communities have involved meetings, financial aid, friendships, marriages, visitations, migrations of members from one community to another, youth retreats, joint projects for pursuing God's shalom in the world, and the Valle Nuevo relationship.

Many of the members of Shalom Mission talk about Valle Nuevo as another member of the association, a concept which all of us, both Shalom Mission and Valle Nuevo, realize is a stretch. The difficulty is in essence the great chasm.

THE CHASM

There are some fairly standard ways of crossing the geography that lies between El Salvador and the United States. Many from the south who undertake this journey travel incognito, overland, right through the perils of the chasm. If they are among the fortunate who survive this odyssey, they become "illegal aliens" upon their arrival and are rudely greeted with fear, suspicion, and outright rejection. Most who travel the other direction—from north to south—fly above the land, literally and figuratively jetting over the chasm, oblivious to its obstacles of borders, politics, cultures, centuries of imperialism, and language. These people are typically traveling for business, for pleasure, or for benevolent endeavors such as mission trips or development projects.

Even though the geography may be traversed, there remains a social, political, and spiritual chasm. Despite the positive interactions, meaningful engagements, or short-term affiliations that result from these occasional encounters, the chasm itself is undisturbed, its vacuity unfilled, its iniquity unchallenged, its authority to define, delineate, and ultimately divide still unquestioned. To understand the true nature of this chasm we have turned to Scripture.

In a series of radically challenging economic parables recorded in Luke 16:19–31, Jesus told the story of two men, one rich and one poor. The rich man, dressed in purple and fine linen, lived lavishly and selfishly and

INTRODUCTION

ignored Lazarus, the poor man, who sat destitute, hungry, and ill outside his gate. Both men died, and in an ironic reversal Lazarus was carried away to rest with Father Abraham while the rich man found himself in Hades tormented by flames.

In constant agony, the rich man looked up to Abraham and begged for mercy, for just a drop of water from the finger of Lazarus to cool his parched and burnt tongue. Abraham, though, declared that what had come to pass was irreversible. While the rich man was receiving good things during his lifetime, Lazarus had only "evil" things. With complete finality, Father Abraham concluded, "Between you and us a great chasm has been fixed, so that those who might want to pass from here to you cannot do so, and no one can cross from there to us" (v. 26).

The rich man raised his voice and pled for Abraham to send Lazarus to warn his five brothers "so that they will not come into this place of torment" (v. 28). Abraham, however, was firm: if his brothers would not listen to the prophets, they also would not be convinced by someone rising from the dead. The chasm was deep, evil, and permanent; it was a nonplace of oblivion for the rich man who subsequently was to remain nameless throughout the millennia. His opportunity to see the image of God in Lazarus and thereby fill the chasm was forever gone.

The metaphor is fitting; the chasm between Valle Nuevo and Shalom Mission is great. While the most visible aspects of the division—language, culture, and religious traditions—are benign, it has a far more insidious reality. Material wealth is concentrated inside the gate on the north side of the border, while in the south privation is a daily reality. In political power, the north has a monopoly. Those from the north can come and go as they please, visiting El Salvador with no special permission, just as the rich man could travel back and forth through the gate. Those from the south are stuck outside the gate with Lazarus.

The genesis of our chasm can be traced back to the conquests, wars, and rebellions of the colonial period that eventually resulted in the creation of nation states in the North American continent. While others might debate this point, we—those of us from SMC and from Valle Nuevo—agree that the history of our two countries is a one-sided story of imperialism and economic exploitation.

The Salvadoran civil war and United States foreign and economic policy in recent decades have increased the profoundness of our separation. On one side are the financiers of war; on the other side are its victims. On one side are those who have benefitted greatly from access to less expensive goods through "free trade" agreements; on the other side are those with a diminished hope for a viable local economy. Those on the north side of our chasm feast in purple robes, while those on the south beg and are covered in sores.

In the first fifteen years of our relationship a few people from Valle Nuevo were able to secure a visa and visit the Shalom Mission communities and attend its large biannual reunions, but then for ten years there was a de facto prohibition of *campesinos* traveling north due to the U.S. Consulate's interpretation of economic sufficiency requirements regarding visas for Central American visitors. After significant lobbying efforts with the consulate in San Salvador, one Valle Nuevo delegate was able to attend the 2015 SMC gathering in Waco.

In the profound depths of this chasm, tenacious and pernicious stereotypes, deeply rooted in our subconscience, grow unabated. "Be very careful in these relationships," goes the conventional wisdom of the north, "because what the Central Americans really want is our money." And the distrust of the south, "All the *gringos* care about is money and exploiting the *campesinos*," has been validated by previous generations of experience.

The chasm also has its psychological dimensions. Shalom Mission members, as United States citizens, carry a sense of guilt about unmerited privileges and a feeling of complicity in the persecution and exploitation of the people of Valle Nuevo. Conversely, as is often the case with those who have suffered, the residents of Valle Nuevo are subject to a deep-seated sense of inferiority and inadequacy when they are with the more affluent. Crossing the chasm to form a relationship with such heavy emotional baggage is part of this story.

THE TRANSNATIONAL COMMUNION

Beginning with the negative may help explain the nature of our relationship. There is no missional call to an endeavor that posits benefactors or evangelists on one side and the destitute or the unredeemed on the other. God's beneficence and grace are resident in Valle Nuevo as well as the Shalom Mission communities.

We do not provide exposure trips for individuals traveling from one country to the other so they can return as enlightened individuals to life and business as usual. While all of us have had our personal horizons expanded,

Introduction

the collective aim of our travels and visits is to extend our experience of community and live as people of *shalom*.

Our relationship is not defined or driven by a commitment to development on behalf of those who need empowerment. Later chapters share an explanation and stories about the work in Valle Nuevo of World Hunger Relief and Habitat for Humanity of El Salvador that has been spawned by our relationship, but these projects are an organic outgrowth of the friendship, not its aim or its justification.

When our communities are together, we do not preach, we do not serve, and we do not work. Instead we do what friends and family do when they are reunited; we sit, visit, and eat. If there is any work going on, it is just to get prepared for a party and clean up afterwards.

The Spanish word '*compañeros*' works well to describe who we are to each other. We are companions; we walk alongside each other. There is a long tradition within Central American resistance movements of *acompañamiento*, standing in solidarity and accompanying each other through a journey of suffering towards redemption. '*Compañero*'—literally 'sharing bread' in Spanish—reminds us that everything we possess is held for the common good.

We do not call ourselves a community for the obstacles to community in our situation are profound, monumental, and numerous: the distance between us is too great, the frequency of our visits too seldom, and the presence of the chasm yet too real. "Communion," however, has emerged as an alternative to explain the joy, kinship, forgiveness, and healing we experience in this relationship.

This choice may seem odd since our communities come from radically different traditions in theology and administration of the Eucharist or the Lord's Supper. The people of Valle Nuevo are Catholic; the Eucharist for them must involve the ministry of a priest. The Shalom Mission communities, on the other hand, are primarily Anabaptist and for the most part believe that any meal involving two or three or more Christians holds the potential of being the Lord's Supper.

In the New Testament, however, communion was not just a ritual or a meal but rather the state of spiritual unity among very diverse communities and peoples brought together by their confession of Jesus Christ as Lord. "Welcome one another, therefore, just as Christ has welcomed you . . . " the Apostle Paul wrote to members of vastly different Gentile and Jewish traditions of the Christian communion in Rome. For this, their acceptance of each other, would be "the glory of God" (Rom 15:7). Paul's exhortations to forgive and seek unity had sociological ramifications for the very diverse first century Christian communities in the Roman Empire. Herein we find encouragement, guidance, and validation of our efforts at reconciliation and community building.

Our differences truly are an opportunity. Communion as a spiritual reality transcends time and space; communion can span a chasm. We are *compañeros* in a transnational communion.

Particularly relevant to our communion is Paul's instruction to the church in Corinth about their agape meal. The Corinthian fellowship was plagued with social and spiritual chasms. The wealthy claimed special privileges; classism stifled their gatherings; and division, arrogance, and scorn, rather than faith, hope, and love, characterized their feasts. "Wait for one another" (1 Cor 11:33), Paul urged the Jews and Gentiles, males and females, slaves and free, who gathered in the name of Christ. Dispense with the factions, the hierarchy, and the stratification of the godless society surrounding you. For when you come together to eat, it is the Lord's supper.

Paul's exhortation crescendoed as he reminded the brothers and sisters of how Jesus celebrated his last supper with his disciples. This passage is now known as the "words of institution" and is used worldwide as Christians celebrate the Eucharist.

> For I received from the Lord what I also handed on to you, that the Lord Jesus on the night when he was betrayed took a loaf of bread, and when he had given thanks, he broke it and said, "This is my body that is for you. Do this in remembrance of me." In the same way he took the cup also, after supper, saying, "This cup is the new covenant in my blood. Do this, as often as you drink it, in remembrance of me." For as often as you eat this bread and drink the cup, you proclaim the Lord's death until he comes.
>
> (1 Cor 11:23–26)

Five themes or movements materialize in this passage:

- Suffering: *on the night he was betrayed*
- Giving thanks: *and when he had given thanks*
- Sharing: *this is my body that is for you*
- Remembering: *do this in remembrance of me*
- Proclaiming: *for as often as you do this you proclaim the Lord's death until he comes again*

Introduction

Suffering. Giving thanks. Sharing. Remembering. Proclaiming the Lord's death. As we've considered this passage, we've realized our stories reflect these themes. More than themes, they actually have become practices, even unconscious habits, which may seem strange, especially for suffering. They are, so to speak, the bread and butter, the *pupusas* and *curtido* (staples of an everyday meal for the Salvadorans), the loaf and cup of our transnational communion.

"Transnational" also deserves a word of explanation. During the nineties, social sciences began to use the term 'transnational' to explore how migration changes individuals and communities. Transnationalism understands that migration is not merely a movement from one location to another but rather that "the very process of crossing borders creates new social and cultural patterns, ideas, and behaviors."[2] Whereas "international" concepts may draw more attention to exclusivity such as cultural differences and national borders, Ann Miles suggests transnationalism emphasizes the connections fostered between locations, cultures, and individuals.

The research today on transnationalism continues to explore the dynamic connections between migrant communities and their home countries, as well as the relationships between social movements and solidarity groups in different countries. Héctor Perla, a political scientist in Latin American and Latino studies, discusses the uniquely transnational nature of Salvadoran-North American solidarity movements in *Monseñor Romero's Resurrection: Transnational Salvadoran Organizing*. He explains that historic and current Salvadoran solidarity organizations have avoided the ethnic-lobby model of political mobilization and forged truly transnational, multiracial, and multicultural alliances with Salvadoran Americans and non-Salvadoran Americans. In these alliances, each party plays an important role.[3] We did not set out to be "transnational," but we have realized that this currently in vogue term describes our relationship and may help others understand who we are.

THE TABLE OF CREATION

The last supper was only one of many meals Jesus shared with his disciples during the three years they traveled together. The prominent events of his life—a scripture-reading in Nazareth's synagogue inaugurating his ministry,

2. Miles, *From Cuenca to Queens*, 8.
3. Perla, *Monseñor Romero's Resurrection*, 25–30.

turning his face to Jerusalem for his ultimate confrontation with religious and political authorities, walking on water, upsetting the money-changers' tables in the temple, praying in the garden of Gethsemane, and certainly dying on the cross of Golgotha—are pivotal moments in the gospel narrative, but the quintessential scene of his ministry is the common meal. He loved to fellowship. He sat at the table, not just with his disciples, but with all types of people including tax collectors, harlots, and Pharisees. Several of his notable parables were about feasts and banquets, wonderful celebrations to which all were invited (Luke 14:13; Matt 22:9). The realm of God was nowhere more visible than at the table with the brothers and sisters eating together.

The early Christians continued this tradition as the believers of the first church took meals with "glad and generous hearts" in the homes of Jerusalem (Acts 2:46). And in all of the little Jesus communities that proliferated across Asia Minor the adherents of this faith—a faith that insists that all walk on level ground—gathered regularly for agape-love feasts.

In the fullness of time the banquet table will be set, and there will be a place for everyone. The *campesinos* of El Salvador have captured the spirit and promise of this messianic feast in a song that is now a staple of the Salvadoran Mass and has become their popular anthem.

Vamos Todos al Banquete/Let's Go Now to the Banquet

Vamos todos al banquete,	Let's go now to the banquet,
A la mesa de la creación,	To the table of creation,
Cada cual con su taburete	Where each one with their own chair
Tiene un puesto y una misión.	Has a place and a mission to share.
Hoy me levanto muy temprano,	I will rise in the early morning,
Ya me espera la comunidad;	The community's waiting for me;
Voy subiendo alegre la cuesta,	With joy I'm walking up the hill,
Voy en busca de tu amistad.	Looking forward to your friendship.
Dios invita a todos los pobres	God invites all the poor
A esta mesa común por la fe,	To the common table of faith,
Donde no hay acaparadores	Where there are none hoarding the harvest
Y a nadie le falta el conqué.	and no one will be in need.

Introduction

> *Dios nos manda hacer de este mundo* God charges us to make of this world
> *Una mesa donde haya igualdad;* A place where all are equal in love.
> *Trabajando y luchando juntos,* We work and struggle together,
> *Compartiendo la propiedad.* And share everything we have.

This hymn communicates our ecumenical vision of fellowship and our hope for a new humanity. It has become the theme song of our relationship. It is frequently heard during delegation visits and regularly sung in Spanish in all of our communities both in El Salvador and in the United States.

We do not take table fellowship for granted, nor is it easy for us. To sit at the table together we've had to overcome centuries of an intractable master-servant dynamic in which *campesinos* waited on their *patrones* (the landowners) and then later ate apart. Now, no moment is more poignant nor more symbolic of the crossing of the chasm than our sitting at the table taking a meal together. In Christ we pass the plate of *pupusas* from one to another, not as those who dwell south or north of the border, not as communitarians or *campesinos*, and not as those who have funded war or been its victims, but simply as fellow human beings.

We remember the past, but we do not dwell in it. We are not trying to recover some lost moment of innocence, nor or we striving to return to a state of being before sin and separation. We are looking forward to what Christ is doing and will bring to completion. The Apostle Paul in his famous passage about the ministry of reconciliation put it this way, "So from now on we regard no one from a worldly point of view. Though we once regarded Christ in this way, we do so no longer. Therefore, if anyone is in Christ, the new creation has come: The old has gone, the new is here!" (2 Cor 5:16–17, NIV)

Many of our stories are of personal discovery and individual redemption. David Hovde, a member of Reba Place, shares his own experience this way.

> At the 2004 SMC conference in Waco I was moved to hear the stories of Doña Tomasa Torres, Salomé Ascencio, and Margarita Avilez as they spoke of their people's suffering during the Salvadoran civil war. Translator Nancy Gatlin encouraged us to ask what it meant to be sister communities with Valle Nuevo. It meant we were interested in what was happening in each other's life. It meant we would write and visit each other. After hearing this, I decided to visit Valle Nuevo in March, 2005.

Two Communities, The Chasm, Communion . . .

We ate dinner in the homes of different families each evening, where they told us their stories of the civil war. I felt trusted and privileged to hear such honest and vulnerable sharing. We participated in the Stations of the Cross march through all the neighborhoods of Valle Nuevo and Santa Marta. At each station the sufferings of Jesus paralleled a point where the people suffered in their flight to Honduras.

When I was thirteen my family moved to Ethiopia to work with the Mennonite Central Committee. I witnessed much poverty. Barriers of culture, language, and privilege were overwhelming to me, and I did not get to know any Ethiopian people on a deep level. I felt strongly the discrepancy between my standard of living and that of others, but I didn't know what could be done about it. Visiting Valle Nuevo was a healing experience for me. We were welcomed deeply into the lives of the people, stayed in their homes, and recognized our common bond.

All of our individual stories contribute to our collective crossing of the chasm. Tomasa Torres, a leader and a prophet of Valle Nuevo with a knack of speaking for the people of both the south and the north, sums it well, "The relationship with the brothers and sisters has brought about a healing of our wounds the past has left us."

The three spiritual metaphors—chasm, transnational communion, and the table of creation—serve as the three sections of *Compañeros*. Section 1, "The Great Chasm," situates the chasm in our specific context with memories of Archbishop Romero that are essential for understanding the spiritual context for both the *campesinos* and the pilgrims from the north. This section also shares more details about the beginning of our joint story.

Section 2, "Practices of a Transnational Communion," uses stories from our visits with each other to describe the five practices we have drawn from Paul's words of institution.

Section 3, "The Table of Creation," summarizes the lessons learned in the last twenty-five years.

Section 1

The Great Chasm

Besides all this, between you and us a great chasm has been fixed, so that those who might want to pass from here to you cannot do so, and no one can cross from there to us.

Luke 16:26

Chapter 1

The Witness of Romero

Therefore, since we are surrounded by so great a cloud of witnesses, let us also lay aside every weight and the sin that clings so closely, and let us run with perseverance the race that is set before us.

Hebrews 12:1

Archbishop Romero keeps watch over the soccer field
from the chapel wall of Valle Nuevo/Santa Marta

Archbishop Oscar Arnulfo Romero's presence in Valle Nuevo of Santa Marta cannot be overstated. His name is on the lips of many in the murmuring of prayers. His words of encouragement are recalled and heard in

Section 1: The Great Chasm

everyday conversations as well as important meetings. His face greets visitors from the wall of the chapel when they first arrive. His likeness gives shape to belt buckles. His portrait keeps vigil over homemade altars.

The spirit of *Monseñor* Romero dwells not only in Valle Nuevo, but has migrated beyond the borders of El Salvador through the rest of the Americas—Central, North, and South—so that he now abides in the hearts and consciences of people around the world. He inspires not only the poor, both rural and urban, but all, who having heard the gospel-call, accompany them. With the leadership of Francis, the first Latin American Pope, the Catholic Church is moving forward to make official Romero's sainthood, an acknowledgement that he daily walks with us in the struggle for justice, liberation, and *shalom*.

In 1977, when Romero was named Archbishop of El Salvador, the current elders of Valle Nuevo were young adults, teenagers, or even children. They have very specific memories of where they were as they listened to his Sunday afternoon homilies.

"When I was fifteen, my dad built a special box on the wall of our house for the radio," Pedro Membreño recalls. "He would play it at full volume when Romero came on. It was La Voz Panamericana, the UCA (Universidad Centroamericana) radio station."

Some didn't own radios but still found ways to hear the message of hope. Juana Lainez and her family would go into town "to an out-of-the way church and listen in the yard to the messages on Radio Venceremos (the underground radio station of the resistance movement)." Others like Margarita Avilez lived on *estancias* where the overlord banned Romero's prophetic message so they had to "go to the hills to hear the word of God."

But even the hills were not always safe, Pastor Torres points out: "We had to turn the volume down low for fear of the *orejas* (literally the ears, that is the spies of the *patrones* and the military that would listen for hints of subversion)."

These details validate the tangible reality and potency of the message, witness, and martyrdom of this man. The archbishop legitimized the poor, giving them a voice and a moral identity. Juana, along with tens of thousands of others, quotes Romero, "Organize yourselves! Walk in solidarity! Do not kill!" The *campesinos* were thereby enfranchised, and all the people of El Salvador and their *compañeros* were empowered.

"He told us that an organized people are a strong people," recalls Tomasa Torres. "He called us to organize, and we do it with our deeds. Romero wasn't fearful; he would shout the gospel in the cathedral."

Pedro puts it simply, "He did not preach with fear." For a people whose timidity was rooted in generations of abuse and brutality, the exhortation to be liberated from fear was startling.

Monseñor Romero's teachings illuminated the Scriptures so the poor could see a way forward. "When I think of Romero," Salomé Ascencio reflects, "I remember the gospel saying, 'the good shepherd cares for his sheep, but the one who gets paid flees when the wolf comes.' Romero's words and witness caused me to commit myself at that time, to not run when the wolf might come. This is what I have done with the help of prayer."

The good Archbishop did not just invite the *campesinos* to the banquet table; he built the table, he spread the table, he prepared the feast that is served upon the table, and today he still humbly waits on the table. He gave them courage, dignity, and hope, and most profoundly of all, he called them into being.

For more poetic language we can turn to the Apostle Peter's explanation of the before-and-after impact of Christ on the gentiles, "Once you were not a people, but now you are God's people. Once you had not received mercy, but now you have received mercy" (1 Pet 2:10). Once the *campesinos* existed in drudgery and fear; but after Romero they walked in courage and hope to the table of creation where everyone has a chair. Before Romero they were chattel, no more than draft animals, a renewable resource that could be propagated generation after generation. Once Romero had spoken to them, they understood they were human beings created in the image of God.

No one expected Romero to be such a pivotal or even significant player in the tumult of the seventies and eighties in El Salvador. A number of priests who were adherents of liberation theology aided the poor and facilitated the organization of politically active and sometimes violent base communities. In an attempt to discourage and further marginalize this group of maverick priests as well as appease the Salvadoran government and military, the conservative leadership of the Church in February, 1977, selected and installed the bookish, even timid Romero as a caretaker Archbishop.

Just a few weeks later on March 12, Romero's friend Rutilio Grande, a priest who had helped organize *campesinos* in the small town of Aguilares, was assassinated along with two parishioners while on the way to evening mass. In response the Archbishop traveled to Aguilares to celebrate mass and minister to the people. He ended up spending a number of hours listening to the stories of the *campesinos*, hearing their suffering, feeling their pain, and beginning to see the complicity of the Church as well as the government in their exploitation.

When the government refused to investigate the murders, Romero protested and refused from that point on to attend any government functions. His conversion was rapid as he moved from being a quietist to a critic of the government and the military. The Archbishop found his voice on the radio and began to challenge the Church to be true to the way of Jesus. His address on May 8 that same year, titled "The Church's Mission," was representative:

> Yes, brothers and sisters, on the one hand they accuse the Church of being Marxist, of being subversive, while on the other hand they want to saddle the church with a theology that lacks immanence, that is to say a disincarnate spirituality, a protestant-like preaching that remains in the clouds, that sings psalms and prays, but doesn't care about temporal realities. These are not Catholics; the Church gets its inspiration from today's Gospel reading: "In this they will know that you are my disciples, that you love one another. . . . Today the Church demands: if you really love God, treat your neighbor well, your employee, those under you, the prisoner. . . . The Church doesn't preach a disincarnate God, rather it preaches a God of love who manifests himself in neighborly love.

Over the next three years, as the violence increased in El Salvador, Romero consistently spoke with a prophetic voice, calling for justice and liberation while condemning the violence of the government and the callousness of the rich. As the internal conflict escalated into a civil war, he relentlessly preached the gospel. He endeared himself neither to the government nor to the religious powers. Before long the Archbishop himself had become the focal point of efforts to shut down the opposition and maintain the status quo.

Meanwhile the United States was supporting the counter-revolutionary effort with funds, training, and personnel. In February, 1980, Romero wrote an open letter to President Carter, asking him to reorient his country's efforts, bluntly pointing out, "Political power is in the hands of the armed forces. They know only how to repress the people and defend the interests of the Salvadoran oligarchy." That same month he also declared in his radio address, "The poor have shown the church the true way to go. A church that does not join the poor in order to speak out from the side of the poor against the injustices committed against them is not the true church of Jesus Christ."

The Archbishop never addressed the poor as victims, as people to be pitied. With his litany of, "Organize yourselves! Walk in solidarity! Do not kill!" he treated the *campesinos* as moral actors. Because of his message the people began to see themselves not just as the "least of these." He helped them shed the heavy weight of inferiority they had carried from just being poor. *Monseñor* Romero won the trust of the people not only with his words, but also with his life. He allowed himself to be loved by the *campesinos*; he sought out their opinions before his sermons. He lived humbly and forswore the privileges and perks of his office. He was an Archbishop of the people. Irvin Alvarado Hernandez, a Christian businessman in San Salvador who provides the in-country transportation for the SMC delegates, recalls "Romero was not bribed with the latest model car, a palace for a house, or money."

On March 23, 1980, Romero directly addressed Salvadoran soldiers in his homily:

> I want to make a special call to the men in the army, specifically the National Guard bases, the police, and the army barracks: Brothers, you are of our people, you kill your own *campesino* brothers and sisters. The law of God—Do not kill—should prevail over the order to kill another person. No soldier is obligated to obey an order that goes against the law of God. It is an immoral order and no one has to comply with it. It is time that these individuals recover their conscience and obey their conscience over sinful orders. The Church, defenders of the rights of God, of human dignity, of people, cannot remain silent in the face of this abomination.
>
> We want the government to take seriously the fact that their reforms are of no good to us if they are stained with blood. In the name of God, in the name of this suffering people whose cries rise to heaven, more and more tumultuously every day, I beseech you, I beg you, I order you in the name of God: Stop the repression!

The next day as he was celebrating the Eucharist at Divina Providencia, the hospital where he had a small house, the Archbishop was assassinated by a sniper's bullet. Six days later as two hundred fifty thousand people gathered on the central plaza of San Salvador for his memorial, a bomb exploded, and then the government troops that were monitoring the event began to fire their guns on the crowd. When the smoke cleared, fifty people had been killed.

Section 1: The Great Chasm

Archbishop Romero's martyrdom was no surprise. He himself had reflected shortly before his assassination, "I have often been threatened with death. I must tell you, as a Christian, I do not believe in a death without resurrection. If I am killed, I shall arise again in the Salvadoran people.... You may say, if they succeed in killing me, that I pardon and bless those who do it. Would, indeed, that they might be convinced that they will waste their time. A bishop will die, but God's church, which is the people, will never perish."

The fulfillment of the Archbishop's words could not be truer as they pertain to the people of Valle Nuevo. In the refugee camp, they learned that the church is not a building of stone belonging to the bishop and to which only the priest has a key. The catechists, lay leaders trained by Romero and his assistants, led in celebrations of the Word, and visiting priests, in the spirit of Romero, addressed them with the term of respect and affection, *compañeros*.

There in the refugee camp the presence of Christ became real, not just in the communion wafer, but in the community as it assembled and as the people organized themselves. Each one, no matter how humble his or her pre-exile station might have been, had a chair, a place, and a calling, had some essential gift to offer in the community's struggle to build a better life. God had come to live with them. Romero's words, "You are the body of Christ," became tangible and real.

Many of those who travel with an SMC delegation to Valle Nuevo are already familiar with some parts of Romero's story; those who aren't, are introduced to him through videos and readings. The first couple of days of a visitation are spent in the capital city with visits to some of the Romero sites. His life and story help those from the United States cross the great chasm. Ruth Anne Friesen from Reba writes of his influence,

> Being aware of the great changes that happened within Oscar Romero, I feel encouraged that there is hope for each one of us as changes keep happening around and within. It is significant that he cared so deeply for the common folks and kept encouraging an end to the violence, even encouraging military personnel to disobey orders and listen to a higher voice. He certainly was the voice for the voiceless and help for the hopeless. All of this is encouraging as we strive to listen deeply to others and to our own hearts even as we come to listen more deeply to the mysterious Presence that envelops us in love!

The Witness of Romero

> ### He is Here in Spirit
>
> On the third day of our delegation visit we went to the place where Oscar Romero lived. The emotions were high for me, and the nun gave me a hug and said that Oscar Romero loves you. He is here with us; he is here in spirit.
>
> *Megan Hering, Reba Place Fellowship*

Gabriela Gatlin Colmán from Hope Fellowship reflected in her visit in 2008 on the power of Romero's vision and legacy and how she resonated with his exhortation to the people:

> Paulo Freire, Brazilian educator, philosopher and contemporary of Romero, in an essay identified three types of churches based on their relationship with the oppressed. One church opts for a "neutral" relationship; a second type relates to the oppressed through humanitarian work. Both churches either naively or shrewdly preserve the status quo by working to transform hearts but not the social structures that make those hearts sick. The third church, the prophetic church, apprentices itself to the poor, dies to the ideology of domination, and resurrects on the side of the oppressed. Unlike the naïve and shrewd churches, the prophetic church promotes liberation, offers hope, and seeks radical social change in the structures of domination.
>
> At the central cathedral in San Salvador on Sunday morning we encountered one church building, but two churches. Unfortunately, we arrived too late to attend the popular mass. As we walked down the steps to the basement where the popular mass is held near Romero's crypt, we realized we were too late for the main event. We did, however, see the congregation stacking the plastic chairs and storing ten-foot tall rainbow colored feathers that must have had some role in the mass. Everyone had a job to do, the priest worked with several men and women to clear the stage and the altar, families gathered up the chairs, gregarious nuns attended to people in the crowd, and everyone eventually spent a few moments beside Romero's crypt. It seemed that the people here belonged to each other and the work they shared.

In recent years there were many places in El Salvador—on posters plastered on public walls, in images stenciled on t-shirts and above doorways, on a banner in the plaza of Santa Marta—where the silhouette of

Section 1: The Great Chasm

the Archbishop was joined by that of Ché Guevara, the Argentine Marxist who exported his violent, ruthless revolution to Cuba, Bolivia, and other countries. For the elders of Valle Nuevo, who see the *Monseñor* as El Salvador's homegrown saint, as well as those from SMC, with their nonviolent, Anabaptist orientation, it was a discordant juxtaposition.

For many of the youth, though, the two were naturally paired as symbols of unyielding resistance to the powers of oppression. They would use practically the same words—an influence on our community, a guide, an example, a leader in the struggle against the power structure and the fight against injustice—to describe either Romero's legacy or Ché's myth. It is no surprise, however, considering Romero's Salvadoran identity and the probability of his canonization, that over time these murals have not been repainted as they have faded and the t-shirts not been replaced as they have tattered.

More important than Romero's nationality or his validation by the Catholic church, though, is the enduring nature of his vision of the redemptive power of suffering and the unity of all people. All human beings, including the youth, are drawn to the hope that the uncrossable chasm will be crossed, that the table of creation will be set for everyone. Yessica, the daughter of Pastor and Rosa Torres, spoke several years ago of the Archbishop's influence on her,

> I never saw him in person, since I wasn't even born, but my parents have imparted in me his great influence. Romero called us to justice and living out of God's laws in our relationships. I have appropriated his thinking and want to follow his teachings. Romero was for justice and the well-being of all the people. He was a leader who sheltered the people. . . . He left a deep imprint on all of El Salvador. I know that my parents are comforted when they listen to him. No matter what I may do, I know that Romero is influencing me to search for peace, beginning with family. I teach children workshops and try to pass on to them the same values. Romero gives us hope. He was able to transmit it, and the people felt support.

Yessica has since gone on to earn her nursing degree and is providing infant health care in rural pueblos in the department of La Libertad. On weekends she returns to her daughter and husband, her parents, and her community in Valle Nuevo.

Atilo Velis Lainez, another of the youth who was able to study at the university, gives credit to the Archbishop for his desire to return to Valle

Nuevo and make his contribution to the community: "*Monseñor* Romero would tell us that God is not in the sky, but that he is on earth and lives in each of us. Therefore, since God exists, kindness is in all of us. He would tell us that we don't get to heaven by praying but by sharing kindness with all people. That is why our dream is to help others from the community who have not had the same opportunity that we've had to study in the university."

It is the grace of God that El Salvador was given a spiritual presence at a critical point in its history, a human being who did not volunteer for the job and was not seeking a position of importance, a saint who found divine courage to speak boldly to the powers, a scholar who was able to join humbly with the oppressed, and a believer who had the great gifts of faith, hope, and love.

Nancy Gatlin and others of SMC have reflected on the inspiration provided by *Monseñor* Romero for those living in the United States.

> In the same spirit as Martin Luther King, Ghandi, or Helder Camara, his openness to God's truth and his willingness to let truth take him on an unanticipated path, challenges me to explore and wrestle with God's calling to truth in my daily context. As a leader of his people, he teaches me the importance of empowerment rather than re-victimization. He called the *campesinos* to organize as a sacred duty. That collective, communal understanding of the Salvadoran people is an experience that those of us in Christian communities in the states yearn to embody.

God's gift in the person of Oscar Arnulfo Romero cannot be contained by one country. His spirit is the universal witness of God's love; his legacy is a proclamation of gospel hope. As one Valle Nuevo youth poignantly surmised, "*Monseñor* is a promoter of the theology of liberation, a human man with a great sense of humanity for the neediest people; a fighter for the just causes and firm on issues of human dignity. *Monseñor* is an example to follow of how God really wants us to live in peace on the earth, without injustices or violations of human rights."

When the chasm seems overwhelmingly immense and timelessly permanent, and we are subject to the immobilization of despair, it is helpful to draw from the spiritual endowment left for us by the life and message of Oscar Arnulfo Romero. Vilma Recinos, a young journalist whose determination and passion have inspired many other young adults to live and to lead in Valle Nuevo, testifies to his importance for all of us.

Section 1: The Great Chasm

When I feel low, when I feel the world is slipping through my hands, when I see on one of the crosswalks of our country an indigent with lowered countenance and extended hand asking for a few coins or a dollar, I see you—suffering—because your people are still dying of hunger in plain sight of those who are indifferent and have so much....

I clasp your spirit hoping to find a reason to continue living in this country that seems to sink into social violence. I search for you when I feel alone, when I'm fearful, when I am discouraged about a much yearned for peace. I also look for you when I'm happy, when I'm sharing with my friends, when I hear your voice that is heard in your recorded homilies....

Chapter 2

Beginning a Friendship

*I thank my God every time I remember you,
constantly praying with joy in every one of my prayers for all of you.*

PHILIPPIANS 1:3–4

One of the early SMC delegations is welcomed by Valle Nuevo

Section 1: The Great Chasm

A TRIP ACROSS THE chasm to find new friends is not an easy, ten-minute stroll along a familiar path.

"*¡Están perdidos!*—You are lost!"

The legless man in his wheelchair hoisted himself over the threshold, emerging from his tiny, darkened house as though an emissary sent from the very pit of the chasm. With beads of sweat forming on his enormous forehead he shook his grizzled mane, pointed his forefinger toward the underworld, and thundered, "*¡Están perdidos!*" His arm slung forward, pointing down the road in the direction the van was headed, "*¡No hay un camino adelante!*—There is no way forward!"

The journey from the capital of San Salvador to Valle Nuevo of Santa Marta should take about two and one-half hours by car or van, or on a series of buses maybe up to four hours. The last leg, beginning in the municipal seat of Victoria, is a bumpy, bone-rattling ride up a mountain road of stone and dirt or mud, depending on the season, with occasional paved stretches of no more than fifty yards where the earth had washed away during some tropical storm. That last forty-five minutes, though, for the annual Shalom Mission delegation is filled with the expectation of friendship.

Delegates who have made multiple trips to Valle Nuevo are returning to renew relationships that have brought healing, understanding, and mutual support for many years. For the first-time delegates, despite all of their preparations through readings, discussions, and a two-day acculturation in the capital city, there is an inevitable nervousness about an adventure into the unknown mixed with their anticipation of new friends-to-be-made.

But on this delegation trip in 2008, the excitement had turned into frustration and the expectation of community had been replaced by a sinking sense of futility. The newly-contracted van driver from San Salvador, Marcos, had never been to Valle Nuevo. After passing through Victoria and having to choose one unmarked fork in the road over another, he began to stop periodically and ask *campesinos* or other travelers standing in their front-yards, "*¿Es este el camino a Santa Marta?*—Is this the way to Santa Marta?"

Politeness required a positive answer. Everyone responded, usually with a slight hesitation, "*Sí, sí*—Oh yes. *Recto, recto*—Straight ahead. *Adelante en el camino*—It's just down the road." With all of this assistance, the last half-hour of the trip had stretched into two hours. The returning delegates in the van were of no help; one turn looked just like the other, everything was green and familiar. After about the tenth set of go-straight-ahead advice, this one coming from a walker who forty-five minutes earlier had pointed one direction but now pointed the opposite, Marcos threw up his hands in exasperation, stopped the van in the middle of the road, cut the engine, and hung his head.

At that point, emerging from a darkened doorway in a house next to the road, the goliath in his chariot appeared. He hoisted his wheelchair over the threshold and rolled forward into the dirt front yard of his home.

"*¡No hay un camino adelante!*—There is no way forward!" he thundered. Pointing down the road in the direction the van was headed, he shook his finger no. In a rumbling, bone-penetrating voice that rattled the van he continued, "*¡Allá está Honduras!*—That's Honduras."

All eyes in the van stared forward in disbelief; everyone understood "Honduras." It was a dark moment. The delegation knew that the Valle Nuevo community had prepared lunch and was waiting for them, but was there no way to get there? Maybe Father Abraham had been right, the chasm was uncrossable.

Then the oracle turned back and peered into the very soul of those sitting in the van. He swung his arm back around, pointing in the opposite direction from which the group had come, shook his massive head, and boomed, "*¡Regrésen!*—Return! *¡Vuélvanse!*—You must go back!"

There was a pause; the worst of nightmares seemed true, Valle Nuevo was an impossible destination. Margarita Avilez, who was born eighty-three years ago on one of the *estancias* in this part of Cabañas, tells another story of disorientation along the trails and in the hollows of these mountains. Despair nipped at the heels of the *campesinos* when they fled along dark paths from the indiscriminate death brought by guns, bayonets, and fires. Even for those who had grown up in the area one path began to look like another, and they were left to wonder if the death squad was in front of them or behind them. She, however, tells of a pillar of light that appeared, proceeding ahead of them, showing the way and giving evidence that God was guiding them even through the valley of death. Hope was not lost.

With finger still pointing, the giant in the wheelchair concluded, "*El camino a Santa Marta está sobre esa colina.*"

Marcos nodded and sighed with relief, "*Muchísimas gracias, señor,*" and started the engine. The English-only van-riders were bewildered, "What just happened?"

Section 1: The Great Chasm

Someone who spoke Spanish explained, "He said this is the road to Honduras, the road to Valle Nuevo and Santa Marta is the one we didn't take just back beyond the hill."

This strange man, as though from another time and place, was this delegation's pillar of light. Guidance—whether through the valley of death or across a chasm that seems to make community only a fantasy—is a gift from God.

As Marcos turned the van there was silence while everyone shifted emotional gears and backed away from the spiritual precipice, the godless doubt that this was not going to end well. The chasm itself is not godless. St. Teresa of Avila, who kept her faith while traveling through dark nights of the soul, maintained, "The feeling remains that God is on this journey too."

Even if there is no map with a highlighted route and even if the forks in the road are unmarked, conflict may compel us to flee from what has been the familiarity and security of our home and take the first step down into the chasm. For both the people of Valle Nuevo and Shalom Mission Communities, the provocation was found in El Salvador's civil war. For each their continued residence above meant death, physically or spiritually or both; the descent into the chasm was the pursuit of life.

On the Salvadoran side the roots of the war stretch back to the initial Spanish conquest that resulted in the subjugation of the indigenous people by a few wealthy families who owned all of the land and controlled the military and a state church. This feudal hierarchy was bolstered by the church leaders who taught the masses the virtue of submission.

Each generation in that long history spawned resistance movements. In the seventies, the initiative for renewal came from within the Catholic Church itself as some priests and others working with grass-roots leaders among peasant and urban poor came to see the struggle for liberation through the biblical lens of the children of Israel escaping their bondage in Egypt for the promised land. God listens to the cries of the poor and takes the side of the oppressed. For a few years, in the spirit of Moses, Archbishop Romero gave voice to the struggles of the poor for justice, for land, and education, as well as the right to organize solutions to their needs as befits the dignity of human beings created in God's image.

Not only did liberation movements regularly emerge in El Salvador's long history of suffering, they were also all met with bloody repression. Romero was not alone in his martyrdom; other leaders who took hope from his message met a similar fate at the hands of death squads in a massive military repression. Before long the government branded entire regions of the country as guerrilla-infested rebel-strongholds and began its scorched-earth campaigns. The 1981 massacre at the Lempa was one of these military operations.

The terror brought by helicopters above, blood flowing around them, and swirling, high waters in front of them, was commemorated by the survivors once they had arrived in the Honduran refugee camps in songs and embroidered tableaux in stark detail: soldiers closing in from both the Honduran and Salvadoran sides of the river; people lying broken under the rocks; bodies floating down the rivers; and firepower raining from above.

There were martyrs who sacrificed their lives for others and heroes who placed themselves in danger to help others swim across. There were also angels such as Yvonne Dilling who happened by the grace of God to be at the edge of the river just as the thousands of fleeing *campesinos* arrived. Yvonne, a champion swimmer in high school, was not just a lifesaver but also a witness to the atrocity of the slaughter of fifty individuals as well as the miraculous deliverance of almost four thousand who were able to escape to Honduras.

Stateside a resistance movement had already begun to form in response to the active involvement of the United States government in the civil war. With a paradigm of the Cold War and a justification of "preventing the spread of communism," the United States was investing more than a million dollars a day to build a corrupt military in El Salvador. For activists in the states a deeper understanding of the nature of the conflict was aided not only by reports from internationals such as Yvonne, who were on-site in the conflict, but also by a growing consciousness of the presence in their own country of half a million Salvadorans who had fled the genocide, the heartless recruitment of child-soldiers, and the generalized violence of the war. Many of these refugees were caught on the southern fringe of the United States by the Border Patrol and deported en masse by the Immigration and Naturalization Service (INS, later to be renamed Immigration and Customs Enforcement or ICE), back to the threat of death they had fled.

In response to this brutal policy and refusal of the United States to recognize these refugees' rights to asylum, the Sanctuary Movement emerged, highly publicizing a few refugee families and their host churches that turned their meeting houses into literal sanctuaries, defying the INS to invade the churches and arrest both hosts and guests. However dramatic

Section 1: The Great Chasm

and needed, this prophetic action was no help to those who were already in detention camps awaiting deportation.

In 1983, as part of a Good Friday drama, Julius Belser a leader of Reba Place Fellowship stood as Pontius Pilate and washed his hands, symbolically absolving himself of any responsibility for Jesus's execution. Julius, haunted by this role, recognized it was impossible as a United States citizen to escape complicity in the miscarriage of justice that was resulting in the pending deportation of thousands of Central Americans held in detention centers.

Julius came up with a bold plan that would take advantage of Canada's recognition at that time of most Central American refugees as legitimate asylum seekers. It would come to be called the "Overground Railroad," named after the Underground Railroad that mysteriously spirited escaped slaves to safety and freedom in Canada before the American Civil War.

There were several essential parts to the network of cooperation. Reba Place sent Richard and Ruth Anne Friesen to south Texas as anchors for a team of interviewers who visited refugees in shelters and INS detention centers, determining those who were most in danger, and then assisting them in making application for asylum in the states. With their deportation proceedings temporarily frozen, they were then bonded out of detention at a thousand dollars a head and sent with caravans of volunteer drivers to host churches farther north.

In Comer, Georgia, Jubilee Partners, a Christian community with its Año de Jubileo (Year of Jubilee) bus and refugee welcome center became a main stop on the way to Canada. The Canadian consul in Atlanta interviewed refugees at Jubilee and granted them the promise of asylum in six months when documents and Canadian sponsoring churches would be ready. From Jubilee the refugees moved on to host congregations and eventually to Canada. As they left the United States their bonds were returned and recycled as a revolving bond fund to release other refugees from detention.

From a basement office in Julius's household at Reba Place the Overground Railroad grew to include dozens of drivers, about 120 host churches in the states, and a number of sponsoring groups in Canada. David Janzen, a member of Reba Place who had been mentored by Julius, was recruited into the work of "running a railroad" and before long became its coordinator. Through the eighties this network of volunteers assisted about two thousand refugees in finding sponsors and reuniting with their families.

The Overground Railroad also helped expose the United States policies that demonized the refugees as communists and justified their slaughter and disappearance by military and para-military forces. Meanwhile, the war between the Salvadoran army and the Faribundo Martí National Liberation Front (FMLN), the umbrella group of the guerrilla forces, dragged on to a bloody stand-still.

In 1984 Herald Press published Yvonne's *In Search of Refuge* which told the story of the *campesinos'* exodus and deliverance at the Lempa and their sojourn in the wilderness of refugee camps. In the village of Los Hernández on the Honduran side of the river, *campesino* Christians shared all the food they had, becoming as poor and threatened by Honduran soldiers as the refugees they had taken in. Yvonne's stories and those of other witnesses galvanized churches, volunteers, and international relief agencies to assist about nineteen thousand Salvadoran refugees, helping them to survive in the camps. Many, including those who had fled across the Lempa, eventually ended up farther inland at Mesa Grande, a large camp with some eight thousand refugees.

In the camps, miserable as they were, the scattered refugees learned how to organize and became one people, launching their own schools and forming grass-roots committees to meet every need. When the community came together, whether in a business meeting, a training workshop, the celebration of mass, each one contributed and leadership grew. They met under whatever shade they could find, often a wide-spreading mango tree.

In 1989 the world was appalled by the night-time execution of six Jesuit professors and their housekeeper and her daughter at the Universidad Centroamericana by the elite, United States-trained Atlacatl Battalion. Support for the war was waning in Congress and refugees began to make their way back to El Salvador.

In October of that year, the group that would become Valle Nuevo took down their barracks, put the lumber and tin on United Nations trucks, and made the long trek to Santa Marta to establish their own community of solidarity. This time as they came up the opposite bank of the Lempa River they were met not by bullets and fire, but with guitars and songs of welcome and the amity of Salvadoran Christians. They arrived in their old homeland to build a new community. Their makeshift houses with dirt floors built with scavenged boards and scraps of metal were a testament that the future—when armies would lay down their weapons and the people are no longer victims—had arrived.

Section 1: The Great Chasm

Throughout the war, Yvonne continued her work in Honduras as a friend, supporter, and co-laborer with the refugees. As the war wound down she too moved to rural El Salvador and continued her ministry as a connecting person, helping build relationships between church groups in the United States and the newly settled *campesino* communities.

In 1991 Yvonne, who was on a stateside visit, attended a conference of radical Christian communities in Grand Rapids, Michigan, where she sought out David Janzen. David remembers, "We walked and talked one whole night through. In her soft yet passionate voice Yvonne told about a bold initiative on the part of the Salvadoran refugees from the Mesa Grande camp who had returned and were determined to organize themselves into villages of peace that would be defended by the means of peace back in El Salvador."

"Though they did not use theological language in Yvonne's relating of their story," David reflected, "I was struck by the image of eschatological villages in precarious vulnerability and with international support living the peaceful and fruitful future that God intends for them. No matter what the powers of the age might say." Yvonne throughout that night continued to tell David about the inspiration brought by these friends as they lived courageously through hardships. David heard God's voice as well that evening, and a vision began to emerge. Could the Overground Railroad, in addition to helping refugees find asylum in a strange land, become an organization that supported communities of refugees in finding sanctuary on their own soil?

Yvonne's plea focused on the particular village of Valle Nuevo, the third group to return from Mesa Grande to the Santa Marta area. They had no international sponsors or network of wider solidarity. This community of about nine hundred souls, about 150 families, had settled just across the road from the first two encampments of returnees to Santa Marta. When David arrived back home he began to arrange for a delegation of adults and teens from Reba Place and Plow Creek to make a first visit to Valle Nuevo.

Meanwhile the United States ambassador to El Salvador, inspired by the story of the five thousand refugees who had returned to northern Cabañas during war-time, demanded peace. He traveled into "enemy territory," as defined by the Salvadoran government, to visit the people of Santa Marta and recruit their support for a negotiated settlement to the conflict. He asked the Santa Martans to appeal to the guerrillas to lay down their arms while he brought pressure on the Salvadoran military to institute a cease fire. The people of Santa Marta countered, "Can you get us electricity?" He promised, and that sealed the deal.

The first SMC delegation landed in El Salvador on January 16, 1992, unknowingly the very day the United Nations-brokered Peace Accords was signed. The whole country erupted into celebration. The delegates joined half a million Salvadorans jubilantly crowding into San Salvador's central *Plaza Nacional*. Every tree and statue was covered with bodies climbing high into the air, cheering, shouting speeches, and singing songs of solidarity. Politicians speaking from an improvised stage celebrated the Peace Accords and promised that a national police force would be formed from the ranks of demobilized soldiers of both the national army and the FMLN. A downsized army would be no longer used to control and harass the civilian population but rather to defend El Salvador's borders.

The cathedral, draped with a vast banner, was graced with the face of the martyred Archbishop Romero. Busloads of *campesinos* from the countryside, with their children in tow so this historic day would be remembered far into the future, arrived for the event. Red bandanas and t-shirts were worn openly by FMLN party members who had been transformed on that day, by the stroke of a pen, from outlawed and hunted "communists" to a legitimate political party authorized to compete in the next round of elections. The celebration went far into the night; people slept everywhere in the parks.

The morning after the Peace Accords celebration the SMC group joined the central worship where the Archbishop Rivera y Damas welcomed the six leading FMLN generals, "You have always been part of the Salvadoran family." The congregation gave them a standing ovation as the Archbishop continued, "Now we welcome you back among us as civilian leaders who will help to reconstruct a new El Salvador through the election process, rather than through war of which we have suffered enough." Hope suffused the entire country.

The delegation arrived for the first time in Valle Nuevo the evening of January 17. The mini-bus was greeted by barking dogs, hordes of excited children, and a wide banner hung between two poles at the entrance to the soccer field proclaiming, "*Vivan los hermanos que se solidarizan con nuestra comunidad*—Long live the brothers and sisters who are in solidarity with our community." The delegates were regaled with songs of community and friendship, poems composed for the occasion by Tomasa Torres and Lydia

Section 1: The Great Chasm

Hernandez, and speeches from Pastor Torres and other members of the *directiva* delivered through a megaphone.

The hosts led the delegation on a community tour of newly-constructed, dirt-floor homes that Valle Nuevo crews had built for each family with boards and tin salvaged from the Mesa Grande refugee camp as well as the communal kitchens where food was being cooked for nine hundred people until the families each had the means to feed themselves. Ten-year-old Guadalupe and her friends organized all the children and the SMC youth into big circle games that instantly created a common language of friendship.

The SMC delegates, who back home were accustomed to frequent meetings to manage the life and business of their own Christian communities, soon found out as they were ushered into a meeting with the *directiva* that they shared this culture with Valle Nuevo. Members of the *directiva* explained that as a repatriated community they were on a three-step-path of development from survival to subsistence to self-sufficiency. They had survived for a period of time with relief aid from UNHCR (the Office of the United Nations High Commissioner for Refugees), Caritas (a Catholic relief service), and other charitable agencies. They had developed gardens and flocks and had begun to subsist, but they needed their own land to grow food in order to reach self-sufficiency. The delegation was impressed by both their clear understanding of community goals and an array of committees including task teams for education, pastoral care, health, cultural events, housing, and water management.

The next morning the delegates woke to the sounds of roosters crowing, dogs barking, the "put-put" of communal *masa* grinders, and the smell of tortillas cooking over wood fires with hot beans and sweet *campesino* coffee of ground toasted corn. Excited children came and interrupted their breakfast, dragging them by the hand to the *cancha*, the central soccer field, where something very big was obviously about to happen. Hundreds had already gathered and were waiting.

Within minutes a single file of FMLN soldiers, men and women carrying their rifles with red bandanas around their brows, more than two hundred in all, descended from the mountains to the small plain of the *cancha* where they formed smart, straight lines. Blue United Nations Land Rovers arrived, and international observers stepped out to make sure this important moment went right. Over the horizon came a white helicopter that descended in a huge cloud of dust onto the *cancha*, and out stepped one of the FMLN generals along with a UN Peacekeeping Forces Commander to the general applause and cheering of the crowd.

The FMLN General and the UN Commander both made speeches announcing that as of that day the FMLN troops were no longer soldiers but civilians. They could lay down their weapons because their safety was guaranteed by the UN forces. Thus far they had learned to live and survive by their guns, but now there would be classes for them in the coming weeks to teach them a trade. They would receive housing subsidies so they could build their own homes and reintegrate their lives into their communities. There was some tension in the air; some murmured that this good news could not be trusted, that the death squads would arrive in the night and take advantage of their defenselessness, that some from the FMLN had kept arms caches in the mountains, just in case. Mostly, though, there was relief and joy, and celebration carried the day.

Later that morning the *directiva* and a women's group thanked the delegation for their presence. If their enemies knew, they explained, that Valle Nuevo had international solidarity—sister communities in *El Norte*—it would add to their safety. And if anything happened to them, they would trust that the delegates would let Washington, DC, know. Then, David remembers, "They cried, and we cried. We hugged each other. We had no idea that our brief friendship could have such power. Somehow in that moment we knew that God had bonded us together, that we were one people, called to walk together even though the path ahead was unclear." Years later, when the van carrying the seventeenth annual SMC delegation—the one that had been lost in the hills and almost ended up in Honduras—finally topped the last rise and drove down into the valley, the SMC members were greeted with a late lunch, deliciously warmed by the affection of a friendship that long before ceased to be brief.

For the first decade of our relationship we depended on Co-Community Development Association (COCODA) with Tim Crouse as its North American representative to help organize the delegations. Yvonne served as facilitator and translator for many of these events and for ongoing communication between the communities. Yvonne eventually returned to the states, and Nancy Gatlin of Hope Fellowship and Dawn Noelle Smith Beutler of Sojourners became the organizers. Through the decades our relationship has continued to grow, deepen, and mature.

Section 2

Practices of a Transnational Communion

For I received from the Lord what I also handed on to you,
that the Lord Jesus on the night when he was betrayed took a loaf of bread,
and when he had given thanks, he broke it and said,
"This is my body that is for you. Do this in remembrance of me."
In the same way he took the cup also, after supper, saying,
"This cup is the new covenant in my blood.
Do this, as often as you drink it, in remembrance of me."
For as often as you eat this bread and drink the cup,
you proclaim the Lord's death until he comes.

1 Corinthians 11:23–26

Chapter 3

Suffering

The Lord Jesus on the night when he was betrayed took a loaf of bread....
1 CORINTHIANS 11:23

Una Vía Dolorosa—A Stations of the Cross march in Valle Nuevo

THE APOSTLE PAUL'S INSTRUCTION to the fractured fellowship in Corinth for building, repairing, and maintaining unity begins with Christ's passion, "The Lord Jesus on the night when he was betrayed...." Suffering is front and center in the introduction to our narrative; it is foundational in our relationship. It cannot be shunted to the back room and forgotten. In this spirit we begin our set of practices for a transnational relationship with a commendation of suffering.

At the closing *despedida* (goodbye gathering) during the delegation visit, once everyone is satiated with *pupusas* and friendship, it is fairly standard for Pastor Torres to stand and address the SMC delegates on behalf of the *directiva*. "We thank you for coming. It means so much that you travel here and visit with us. We know that you suffer when you are here."

Ouch! Pastor's words usually cause a few SMC delegates to cringe as they recall their whiny moments of murmured complaints to each other—in English—about an outhouse or a cold bucket-shower and contrast them to the stories they have heard over the previous few days of exile and desperation experienced by their new friends of Valle Nuevo.

Angelina Membreño, for instance, in a conversation on her verandah one afternoon shared freely how she submerged herself in the Lempa River for three days in 1981 in order to hide from the death squads. "*Sufrimos demasiado*—We suffered too much," Angelina shook her head, the pain still fresh thirty years later. "*Sufrimos demasiado*," she repeated the refrain as she moved from one chapter of the saga to the next, recalling the hardships she and others had to face in the refugee camps and then in the rebuilding of a community in the Salvadoran countryside.

> ### Suffering Makes a People
>
> Common suffering as refugees fleeing from terror and their faith in rebuilding a common life, have shaped them into a people. . . . What a difference it is to visit with a people rather than just visiting people.
>
> DAVID JANZEN, REBA PLACE FELLOWSHIP

Angelina's cultivated yard is the centerpiece of the Membreño family compound, a group of several homes belonging to their adult children and extended family members. Her garden is full of tropical greens, flaming reds, and brilliant yellows, parrots and other exotic birds, goats, and chickens plus fruits with no known English translations to any of the stateside visitors. Family members come and go with no hurry. In the distance there are other sounds of Valle Nuevo's community life, a dog barking, children at play, and an occasional vehicle climbing the dirt road made invisible by the dense foliage on the hillside.

A sense of peace pervades the Membreño home, but the spirit of suffering is not vanquished by this beauty. Suffering and beauty co-exist with each other, even complement each other, in the same way that wrinkles and graying hair add to the dignity and grace of elders. Suffering in Valle Nuevo is not just a memory; it holds an intimate relationship with each individual regardless of age or generation.

Dawn's Journey of Suffering

As I sit in front of the altar in Divina Providencia where Monsignor Romero was martyred, the faith that I could have lost is restored.

Happiness and joy draw some to an encounter with the divine God, but for me, it is suffering that restores me. To witness suffering, martyrdom, and the capacity of a human being to choose a path that will lead to certain death reminds me that God can move our hearts, distance us from selfishness, and bring us to complete surrender. There we can be surprised by joy, happiness, and peace.

In 2009, when I first visited Valle Nuevo as an SMC delegate, I was coming to the end of my hope for marriage reconciliation. I was aware that in my brokenness I had little to offer these new acquaintances other than my presence and an understanding of the Spanish language that thirteen years in Central America had afforded me.

As I listened to their stories of suffering—stories not only of the horrors of war, but also of infidelity, separation, and single parenthood—I could feel internally my own pain resounding with empathy. I did not anticipate the opportunity to share my own story; my suffering seemed to pale in comparison. But over those few days of conversation as small details of my own life circumstances emerged, this place and this people expressed their solidarity with me and my pain.

Through these stories that cannot be compared but only shared, I received in Valle Nuevo peace and healing.

My own process of suffering and healing, including new pains and joys, has remained ever-present in my mind as I interact with the emotions and stories of my friends in Valle Nuevo. One of my first journal entries during my second visit in 2010 reads: "Feeling energized by being here in Valle Nuevo—ready to share, translate, participate, facilitate. It feels good to be able to give back."

Section 2: Practices of a Transnational Communion

> Rest comes from knowing one has company on the journey through a world of inequality. The pains are the same. The wounds and the hurts in the flesh and in the soul unify us in the image of God that we carry on our face and even in the molecules of our bodies and the essence of our spirit.
>
> > The same sun warms us.
> > The same breeze refreshes us.
> > The same water gives us life and cleanses us of impurities.
> > The same sounds activate our minds.
> > The same smells awaken our hunger.
> > The same food sustains us, and when the elements are lacking,
> > an embrace carries us to a place of refuge where art heals us.
>
> *Dawn Noelle Smith Beutler,*
> *Church of the Sojourners*

After the conversation with Angelina, several of the delegates walked across the front yard to talk with Mari Villalobos, the *compañera* (girlfriend) of Angelina's son Douglas. It was not long before Mari was telling the story of her harrowing experience when she tried to enter the United States.

She was abandoned north of San Antonio by her coyote (an immigration broker and guide), and then lost, hungry, and thirsty, she wandered for a few days before she was picked up by Immigration and Customs Enforcement (ICE). After several weeks in detention she was deported back to El Salvador.

One of the delegates, with a view of Angelina's magnificent garden, asked, "Why, Mari? Why would you leave this place?"

"There are gangs here. I need work. I want to see my *Papi* in California." Words and a sad smile communicated the ubiquitous emotional trauma, relentless poverty, and fractured relationships of her world. The feeling of well-being in this setting belongs to the SMC visitors who bask in its calm as they detox from the overstimulation of their urban setting. The *campesinos* love Valle Nuevo and Santa Marta but are constantly aware that oppression is deeply rooted in their history, that violence is widely spread in their society, and that their local economy is practically nonexistent.

Every year the delegates hear other stories from the Valle Nuevo youth who undertake the journey north despite the hardships of hunger and cold, the high risk of apprehension and detention, and the potential of being robbed, assaulted, or even killed. If they make it, they face not only the debt from what they borrowed to pay the coyote but also the difficulty of beginning an underground life in a new place with strange customs and a foreign language.

So, it is difficult for those from SMC communities to hear Pastor refer to their brief discomfort with the same word that Angelina used to describe the trauma, deprivation, and humiliation the *campesinos* have known for generations. The disparity in intensity, depth, and longevity of the pain felt by the various individuals of our transnational communion stretches the suitability of 'suffering' almost to the breaking point.

In years past, after Pastor had made his statement about the *directiva*'s sympathy for the delegates, one or more of the SMC leaders would object, "Please, Pastor! Suffering? We may never get used to chickens running around our legs during meetings, and some of us, no doubt, will feel a little sick by the time we leave, but these are only inconveniences, the very same ones you experience when you visit us stateside. Our water tastes odd to you. Our smoke alarms can frighten you." This reference to Tomasa's and Margarita's story about their unnerving experience of cooking *pupusas* at the Gatlins' house during their 2004 visit always brings smiles.

> ### How Little We Can Do
>
> It is painful to hear stories of loss, violence, and exploitation of our *campesino* friends, and not be able to do something to fix the situation. Perhaps God is showing us in a new way what it means to be human—how little we can do. How God's heart must ache as he knows the experience of all the suffering in the world.
>
> JIM FITZ, REBA PLACE FELLOWSHIP

But now, after years of learning through this relationship, the stateside visitors have accepted Pastor's characterization of their experience despite the astronomical difference in scale. Suffering is a universal companion; it is ever-present in all human narratives. It finds occasion not only in civil wars, but also in the most local and personal parts of all of our stories.

Section 2: Practices of a Transnational Communion

> ### Bearing Our Burdens Together
>
> My trip to Valle Nuevo last summer marked an important turning point in my "please don't ask me to do that again" attitude. Telling my own story from start to finish seemed too overwhelmingly painful. But the folks in Valle Nuevo have learned to tell an incredibly painful story very well, and while the pain is present, there is also hope. There is sorrow, but there is also joy. In my experience, bearing one another's burdens doesn't necessarily make them lighter, but as God's strength is made perfect in our weakness, we bear our burdens better together, and they do not crush us.
>
> *Dawn Noelle, Church of the Sojourners*

Every human association, even the most uncomplicated of relationships such as a friendship of two, requires forbearance of the personality and idiosyncrasies of the other. By comparison, a transnational relationship provides unlimited opportunities of insensitivity, oversight, miscommunication, misinterpretation, disregard, and offense. One person's unfamiliarity with a local custom of greeting everyone upon entering the room may be interpreted as arrogance or disrespect. Another person who out of shyness or deference does not make eye contact when addressing others may be perceived as sullen or hostile.

Communicating bilingually is itself filled with landmines of offense that clumsiness can detonate. Anyone can learn a few words and make functional use of the present tense in the other tongue, but to be able to employ the words of politeness—the conditional or the subjunctive bolstered by just the right adjective or adverb—is divine, an accomplishment most of us can only hope for in the by-and-by.

More concretely, though, a transnational visit—regardless if it is north visiting south or south visiting north—thrusts people into unaccustomed and discomfiting environments. The guest bed may be too hard or too soft. The night sounds of traffic and trains or dogs and roosters fail to fade into soothing whispers that lead to slumber. Toilet facilities seem exotic and disrupt internal rhythms. The food served at the table, although tasty, is not our usual fare and may leave us with intestinal turbulence. SMC delegates have come to accept that even minor suffering is not shameful or embarrassing and, therefore, should not be denied.

> ### Cross-Cultural Experiences
>
> When I just arrived in Chicago it was like a new world! It was seven pm and still light outside. Everything I saw was most precious. The reception I received was well-planned and coordinated. The strange thing was the food. After three days my stomach hurt. I kept smelling tortillas but couldn't find any. I was sick for a month at Plow Creek. All I could eat was brown rice and lettuce. While at Plow Creek I helped with the harvesting of tomatoes, chilis, and watermelon. I thought it was very strange that the produce was left at a stand with just a listed price and no one to watch the stand. The next day we'd come back and find the money. I also had the scary experience of making tortillas the time that Margarita and I stayed with the Gatlins in Waco. Nancy had gone to work, and I attempted to make tortillas. All of a sudden a loud alarm went off. Margarita was in the shower and I was frantically calling her to help me.
>
> TOMASA TORRES, VALLE NUEVO

Just as betrayal is the necessary beginning for the unity to be found in the Eucharist, just as chasm is the metaphor that describes the current separation we experience, suffering is the front porch or verandah of this relationship. As with the early Christians in Jerusalem, our hearts are glad and generous when we pass the plate of warm tortillas around the circle. Our laughter, our music, and our comical swaying of hips when Salomé and Joe try to dance may seem to banish loneliness, isolation, and despair. But then suffering, as though an ancient grandparent sitting in the forgotten shadows on the margin of our circle, leans forward with gnarled knuckles resting on bony knees. Clearing her throat with a raspy, older-than-death cough, she taps the shoulder of someone in the circle.

In one moment grief is plainly visible in the face of a brother across the circle. In the next our sister to the right shares from her anguish. No pain, whether from south or north, personal or generational, is too large or too small to share. Our heads will bow and shoulders sag as we corporately process what is being said. "*Sí.*" "*Claro.*" "Yes." "Mmm-hmm." Low, throaty utterances, murmured in a uni-tonal language that needs no translation, ripple around the circle, summoning the Spirit as God's love and mercy embrace the group. We are reminded that it is the evening of Jesus's betrayal and the table belongs to him. We are still a beam short from spanning the chasm and arriving at the new Jerusalem.

Section 2: Practices of a Transnational Communion

The archetype of our suffering is in the life of our Lord Jesus Christ who challenged the authority of the political and religious powers and subordinated himself to their brutality and punishment. The messiah who suffered is the progenitor of our circle of good will and humor. There is only one table, not two; the millennial feast of joy is spread upon the passover table of Jesus's suffering. In the passion of the Son of God we are invited to beauty and austerity, to rest and rigor, to laughter and weeping, to celebration and mourning. Our cravings in all their complexity are satisfied by the one loaf and the common cup served at our Lord's table. We will not attempt to thwart our DNA by denying suffering.

The following year after the visit with Mari, about eighteen months after her terrifying and heartbreaking experience in Texas, another conversation revealed that even though changed circumstances could appear to provide relief, a deeper sense of loss or deprivation may well endure. Mari's father had returned from California to El Salvador to live in a community some distance from Valle Nuevo. She did not get to see him that often, ostensibly because of the expense of travel, but the sadness in her eyes acknowledged continued alienation in their relationship. The trauma of war and displacement lingers, torturing the psyches of many and eroding the relationships and structures of family and society.

Mari had become since her return the *acompañada* of Douglas. Dawn, one of the delegation leaders, explained to SMC visitors that the *campesinos* have their own version of community-blessed unions since they lack access to the functionaries of church and state, the institutions that hold the keys to formal marriage.

With a broad smile Mari continued, she had given up her plans for another trip north and gone back to high school. She would, she told the delegates with confidence and optimism, finish her degree and then find work in the field of computer technology. The delegates, though, had already heard stories of the frustrated vocational aspirations of younger adults and knew that Mari herself understood the scarcity of jobs in the undeveloped Salvadoran economy. Everyone present recognized that Mari's bright outlook was actually a prayer for herself that she would not succumb to hopelessness.

As followers of Jesus we do not conquer or eradicate suffering but instead accept it and even count it as a privilege. Weeping with those who weep, having compassion (literally, sharing the suffering) with those who suffer, is how we build community. Suffering is both our ethics (what we do) and our ecclesiology (how we build community).

> ### We Are Not Alone
>
> I felt so welcomed. Even while I was throwing up, six little girls came and sat beside me so I wouldn't feel alone.
>
> MATT REHA, FIFTEEN YEARS-OLD AT THE TIME, PLOW CREEK

This is a profound shift for the theology of many affluent Christians who see suffering as something to be alleviated rather than venerated, cured rather than endured, spurned rather than co-borne. For the people of Valle Nuevo of Santa Marta, though, suffering is a necessary lead-in to any story of redemption, and it is a theme that will recur with many visible peaks and valleys throughout the narrative. They talk about pain and suffering as easily and naturally as the people of SMC talk about the weather, their diets, or their agendas.

> ### Report to SMC from a non-delegation visit in March, 2015
>
> The day before the whole community was sprucing up the area of the road outside their houses for the March 18 procession. The actual setting up of the different stages couldn't happen until the next morning as the animals could have damaged them during the night. Around two the procession started. The two priests, Padre Salvador from the Santa Marta Catholic Church and Padre Luis who was excommunicated from the Roman Catholic Church and currently is of the Church of the Magnificat, carried a banner together.
>
> The procession always ends in a mass. Earlier that day I heard from everyone great sadness and distress that the community would process to a point and then divide into the ones following Padre Luis and those following Padre Salvador. At the dividing place the two priests spoke, and in the end a very reconciling Padre Salvador offered for all of us to go into Santa Marta proper so we would not miss the stations there, and then at the end we would all go back to the church building where a united mass could be held. It was a very poignant and healing moment!
>
> NANCY GATLIN, HOPE FELLOWSHIP

Even though the details of suffering—whether lies, faithlessness, oppression, mishaps, or just the wounds of deterioration left by time's ceaseless gnawing at our heels—may be new, the themes are as old as the hills. Those who have sat in the circle before and are seasoned by the longevity of life realize that every story of suffering is both personal and universal. And every story of suffering helps us cross the chasm.

The people of God have known this throughout the ages. "Blessed are the poor in spirit, for theirs is the kingdom of heaven," Jesus began his beatitudes (Matt 5:3). Suffering, the Apostle Paul told one of his favorite churches, is an honor and a perk, "For he has graciously granted you the privilege not only of believing in Christ, but of suffering for him as well...." (Phil 1:29). "Lord, either let me suffer or let me die," prayed Teresa of Avila noting that life without suffering is life not worth living.

The cross was not a unique event required only of the founder of our faith. Golgotha, the hill where the savior's cross was planted, is a standard stop on the itinerary for all who are on the way. If our salvation must be bought with human accomplishment and effectiveness, then we will find ourselves at the end of the work day in a pit of despair dug deep into our own deficits. On the other hand, if the blessing of the world is received through the acceptance of suffering and the grace of forgiveness, then we will find hope for that day when God will fully dwell with mortals (Rev 21:3).

> ### Paid for in the Blood of the Poor
>
> See the image of a human being crucified on the Banco de Cuscatian skyscraper? In our country, we have economic development but no human development. The economic development is paid for in the blood of the poor.... As Christians seeking the kingdom of God, we see that this system is wrong. Even if we do not have the power to change it, we can nourish another vision and way of living among ourselves. We can remember what we have suffered, and take hope that the God of the Bible is the God of the poor.
>
> TITO GOMEZ, PASTOR OF CORDERO DE DIOS IN SAN SALVADOR, EXPLAINING A FOLK-ART MURAL IN THE COURTYARD OF HIS CHURCH DURING AN SMC DELEGATION ORIENTATION

We are promised that in the fullness of time suffering will be no more, but in the not-yet it is still with us. Suffering is our nativity; it is our identity; and it is our future, at least for a while.

Chapter 4

Giving Thanks

The Lord Jesus on the night when he was betrayed took a loaf of bread and when he had given thanks....

1 Corinthians 11:23–24

Sharing thanks-givings and swapping stories

Section 2: Practices of a Transnational Communion

"Salomé, what are you thankful for?" Nancy asked in Spanish.

It was the Saturday before the stateside celebration of Thanksgiving, 2012, and Nancy and Joe Gatlin, who usually are part of the mid-year SMC delegation, were making a rare second visit that year to Valle Nuevo. They sat with Salomé on the verandah of his Habitat for Humanity home. His wife Felipa and other family members occasionally passed by as the rest of the household went about their routines. Despite the absence of turkeys and autumn leaves, Nancy's question was very natural. Whenever we are together, we often pause to relate our gratitude and count our blessings.

"Salomé, what are you thankful for?"

There was a long silence. There is always a long pause before José Salomé Ascencio responds. Those who don't know him well may wonder if he has understood the question. Those who have spent significant time with him know they are in for a treat, that reflection and composition are in process as he decides how far back and how deep he will go to begin his answer.

> ### I'm Thankful I've Had No Amputations
>
> My hope is for my family and the whole community, that for our children, our grandchildren, and our great grandchildren there will be opportunity. Many people are leaving and trying to go to the States. I was never in favor of our children going to the States.
>
> I have a great love for plants and the animals. I would not want to live in the city. My blood pressure and cholesterol are high. I can't afford to eat well—vegetables and fresh fruit are too expensive.
>
> I'm thankful to God that, even though I have other health problems, I have a whole body. I've had no amputations. I'm thankful for community and for solidarity.
>
> Angelina Membreño, Valle Nuevo

With a hint of a smile, Salomé leaned forward and signaled he was ready. "Sometimes I have good thoughts; sometimes I have negative thoughts. They both come and go," he extended his arms and circled his right hand around his left, "like a record playing over and over."

When Salomé talks he always uses his hands; they move slowly, with deliberation, communicating joy as well as illustrating the metaphors that help impart his wisdom. Nancy nodded for Salomé to continue, but ever the teacher he waited patiently, his hands mimicking a turntable playing a vinyl LP, while he looked for a sign of comprehension from Joe whose personal turntable typically lags two or three revolutions behind due to his marginal Spanish.

Salomé's name, derived from the Hebrew *shalom*, reflects his commitment to peace, justice, and prosperity for his community. He has served as a member of the *directiva* and in other leadership capacities in Valle Nuevo over the last almost-three decades since the return, but it is his gift as an educator that invariably, consistently, like a never-ending record, blesses others. During the refugee years Salomé taught the children in the popular school, although he himself had only completed the second grade. One of his daughters who was able to get a university education, Morena, has followed in his footsteps by returning to Valle Nuevo to help lead educational efforts in the community.

He waited for Joe, who took a few seconds and then with a circular nod and an "Hmm-Hmmm" indicated he was up to speed. Salomé's smile broadened, he cocked his head, and with relish continued.

"It was not easy to live through a war." Joe and Nancy settled in. Beginning his thanks-giving with a recounting of the great suffering of the Salvadoran *campesinos* during the war placed Salomé squarely within the biblical tradition. Jesus's prayer of thanks at the last supper was set within the context of his betrayal. The first Eucharist (Greek *Eucharistia*, gratitude) was held during Christ's passion. And the Apostle Paul counseled the early believers that thanks-giving should flow from their experiences of conflict and their anxieties (Phil 4:2–7).

> ### I've Been Holding on to Him
>
> I was also trying to cross with my young child, and there were some people who had a piece of cork for floating. I put my child on it and was getting ready to get on it to go across with the help of someone else when another person got on it. So my child went on across the river. I was just desperate to get across, but it took three hours before someone helped me go across. I got over there, and I couldn't find my child anywhere. And I started looking everywhere, under rocks, everything. I was afraid that he had drowned in the crossing. It was much later that someone brought him over and said, "I've been holding onto him until you got across." I was so thankful, but it was just a time of terror, trying to get your family across.
>
> FELIPA ASCENCIO, VALLE NUEVO

"When they told me of the death of my brother, I felt it very deeply. The suffering of the war made you feel alone. The war was a time of affliction. I had panic attacks while we were in the refugee camp. I felt caught by the politics of it all. Some tell me I am crazy, but no, I lived through this. It was not a psychosis."

Salomé moved forward and then backward and forward again, around and around, visiting the exodus of Moses and the children of Israel, refugee camps, the beatitudes and several parables of Jesus, numerous Psalms, the visions of Isaiah and Archbishop Romero, St. John's tribulation, and the formation of a new community and agricultural cooperative. All were relevant and essential prerequisites for answering Nancy's question about his thanks-giving. His account of blessings needed to be prefaced by an identification with God's people through the millennia of faith, the horror of the war, the establishment of a new people through the hardship of the return, and the hope for a corporate *shalom* yet to come.

This journey of gratitude was not short. Nancy and Joe listened, marveling at the expanse of Salomé's vision, yet remaining confident he eventually would arrive at a very specific and tangible destination.

The people of our transnational relationship are not strangers to long journeys. Crossing the geography between El Salvador and the United States takes at a minimum several hours of waiting in airport lines and navigating through the bureaucracy of immigration and customs. A trip by ground will take a least a week and can involve months in a detention center if going from south to north. The flight to the Lempa River under the cover of night seemed endless. The exile in Honduran refugee camps was protracted. Establishing a Christian community in the United States or building a new village in the Salvadoran jungle can takes years and even decades.

> ### Coming Home
>
> It felt like coming home. I stayed with Angélica, who spent the summer with us in 1997 and slept in our home. Now she was returning the favor.
>
> JIM FITZ, IN 1997 A MEMBER OF PLOW CREEK

Just crossing from one side of Valle Nuevo to the other can be a journey. Margarita Avilez, who lives in *Las Brisas* (Breezes) neighborhood, so named because it is up the hill where on a hot summer day residents may catch a waft of air, spends hours each day walking up and down the dusty roads and trails of Valle Nuevo. In Valle Nuevo's geography *Las Brisas* is practically a suburb; at Margarita's slow pace it is a thirty-minute downhill walk to the village center where she often goes to participate in worship, *directiva* meetings, community celebrations, literacy classes, the school, the soccer field, the church, or Pastor's and Rosa's house.

The walk back up the hill to her Habitat home will take forty minutes, as long as she doesn't drop in to visit someone else or just stop along the road to chat with others who are walking up or down. Once home, she may sit and rest her feet at the altar that fills practically half of her small living room. There the Virgin Mary and Oscar Romero preside beneficently and serenely reminding everyone—family members, neighbors, as well as aliens from the north—that God is present, always inspiring our gratitude, whether on a daily walk in the community or an occasional trek to martyrdom.

> ### The Altars of Our Lives
>
> We read often in the Old Testament about the Israelites setting up altars unto the Lord. They were sacred places to remember and thank God for God's provisions, salvation, protection, and presence. Perhaps it seems like an ancient custom that we more "sophisticated" and secular Christians don't need. I was struck in this last visit to Valle Nuevo by the prominent place that altars have and play, not only in the church building, but in each home. Margarita's is a prime example.
>
> We may differ in our understanding of how these altars are used, but it is a strong statement to the role of faith and gratitude. Knowing Margarita, I know that this isn't just a piece of "furniture" in her house but a daily reminder of God's presence, a presence that she's been aware of during the fleeing to Honduras, their stay in the refugee camps, and in their return to El Salvador. It speaks to me of a very present, daily awareness of and dependence on God.
>
> So where are the altars in our lives? Do we even think it necessary? How do we remember and express gratitude to God? How do we offer ourselves up to God? We may want to think of altars only as metaphors and yet, it seems we humans are in a great need of tangible, concrete expressions of faith. I fear we fool ourselves in thinking we're above it all.
>
> I've found myself as of late, almost unconsciously, forming an altar space in my bedroom, near my chair where I pray. I have visual objects that remind me of times when God met me in very tangible ways.

SECTION 2: PRACTICES OF A TRANSNATIONAL COMMUNION

> When I face my "altar" I'm immediately reminded of God's goodness and a spirit of thanksgiving fills my heart. And I am thankful for Margarita, for her vibrant, quiet testimony to a life lived with gratitude.
>
> NANCY GATLIN, HOPE FELLOWSHIP

Salomé continued to travel through time, leading us to his thanksgiving; his hands stretched to the future, then pulled back to the past, and then opened, palms up, in front of him as he explained the present. Felipa and Salomé are an unassuming couple whose lives have been repeatedly touched by the long shadows of darkness and death, yet they have grown a family into a large, intergenerational household that shines light and generates peace in their part of the valley. They bring to mind Zechariah and Elizabeth, the long-suffering, wishful husband and wife living in the hill country of Judea who were eventually blessed with the birth of a son, John the Baptist. When Zechariah found his voice after the long-awaited birth, he prophesied in his famous Benedictus,

> By the tender mercy of our God,
> > the dawn from on high will break upon us,
> To give light to those who sit in darkness and in the shadow of death,
> > to guide our feet into the way of peace.
>
> > (Luke 1:78–79)

Meanwhile, the light on the Ascencio verandah had slipped into dusk. Salomé continued to work his way to his benediction, and the glow of Felipa's mud oven provided a gentle illumination as the dark gathered.

"I often sing to myself when I am working or going through the day," Salomé continued. He then sang a few lines from a chorus:

"Even when there are struggles and challenges, I will not leave Jesus."

Salomé paused, looking for and winning Nancy's and Joe's affirmation of the truth of these words. Through the last dozen or so revolutions of his turntable the faint scent of *masa*, a corn-based dough, had grown into a delectable aroma as it was being cooked over the open fire.

"Jesus, after all, came for those who are sick. Those of us who are ill need to keep our eyes on Jesus," Salomé nodded, his hands uplifted, affirming the truth of his own statement.

Marga, another daughter, silently approached and placed a plate in the middle of the table with a mound of tortillas spilling out from underneath a cloth napkin. Stomachs clamored. Salomé raised his eyebrows in delight. His eyes sparkled with anticipation as he lowered and spread his hands, presenting the steaming dish to Nancy and Joe. He was ready for the revelation of his thanks-giving, and the timing was impeccable, perfectly orchestrated by a graceful family.

"During the war, we were without food. But now each day there is a mountain of tortillas on the table. We have all of the tortillas we can eat," he gave an impish, knowing smile. "This is what makes us thankful. God has moved through many different people. We came back here. This is the promised land. We discovered God's marvels here. God provides for the birds of the air. We do not have to worry. For this we are grateful."

> ### Simple Words
>
> These are simple words, but they come from the heart. The only thing I can give you is my friendship and millions of thanks. It is a pleasure for me that today you are eating dinner in my house. For being true brothers and sisters and friends, you will remain in my heart always.
>
> ROSA LILIAN MEMBREÑO, VALLE NUEVO

The rest of the family sat down at the table, and when Salomé had given thanks, all of those present, their hearts filled with gratitude, shared the Saturday evening supper of tortillas, *frijoles*, and *pupusas*.

> ### The Joy of Visits
>
> Repeatedly our hosts thanked us for risking sickness, for traveling horrendous roads, for receiving their simple hospitality, for remembering them. How can I describe the blessing of children climbing into your lap, of dogs falling asleep on your feet, of spontaneous questions about the community's history as triggered by photos from years ago when everyone was younger and things were different.
>
> DAVID JANZEN,
> REBA PLACE FELLOWSHIP

On Sunday morning Nancy and Joe continued their Thanksgiving conversations with a visit to Tomasa.

Section 2: Practices of a Transnational Communion

"*Doña* Tomasa, what are you thankful for?" Nancy asked her.

Tomasa, who typically sits with her head slightly bowed as though she is studying something on her lap, cut her eyes up to ascertain Nancy's intent. Then she squeezed her eyes shut, leaned back, and placed two fingers on her lips, obviously working on an answer. Throughout Valle Nuevo's history Tomasa has carried a heavy load. She lost two sons during the war and a third has never recovered psychologically. Since the return, she has served as an organizational and spiritual leader for the entire Valle Nuevo community while providing meager support for her family by selling *pupusas* in the village center.

After a few seconds, as though she had drawn some spiritual strength from the heavens, she lowered her head and silently surveyed the surrounding world: her new Habitat house, the adjoining old, mud-walled structure where her husband who suffered traumatic stress from the war years was resting, across the yard her daughter's home built with funds earned during various sojourns in the states, the chickens, and the community she cares for so deeply.

Tomasa is an orator. The reedy tenor of her voice will start low and then increase, her speech rises and falls with an artful meter and rhythm that stirs the imagination and brings chill bumps even to those who cannot understand Spanish. She speaks as a prophet, bringing down judgment on the principalities and powers that have oppressed their community while upbraiding the people of Valle Nuevo for their sins and shortcomings that have prolonged their enslavement. And, as with the best of prophets, her message will crescendo with a promise of God's providence and hope for the future. She will always then close with a kind and even mirthful smile, letting her listeners know that even though the message is heavy, God holds us dearly and finds joy in us.

After some preliminaries Tomasa's actual thanks-giving focused on the recent development of the lay-led, weekly worship service that is held in the community chapel. Women, as so often has been the case in the history of Christian communities, have provided the initiative and vision for this movement, but now men, particularly the younger generation, are also participating, helping to lead in prayers and singing. The gathering has brought healing and a spiritual-centeredness that was needed in this repatriated community.

Before she could finish Tomasa was interrupted when Marielos, one of Pastor's and Rosa's daughters, emerged in the clearing at the mouth of the path that comes up through the dense underbrush from her parents' home down the hill. Marielos apologized and then handed the cell phone she was carrying to Joe. He stepped out of the circle so as not to interrupt, but a phone call from the states was so unusual that both Nancy and Tomasa stopped to listen.

It was news from back home. Gabriela, Joe's and Nancy's older daughter, had been trying to reach them for four hours. Joe's one surviving sibling, his brother Bob back in Waco, had died unexpectedly during the night. Joe gasped and struggled to speak. Nancy and Tomasa gathered around him, Nancy hugging him, Tomasa stroking his arm reassuringly, while he experienced the first wave of grief. The words of Salomé from the evening before, immediately came to mind, "When they told me of the death of my brother, I felt it very deeply."

> ### A Great Favor from God
>
> It is a great favor from God to have been placed in the company of such good people.
>
> St Teresa of Avila

With flight changes and arrangements, it took Joe and Nancy another day to leave and begin the long journey back home with a van ride to the capital city. In that twenty-four hours there were many empathetic stories of the pain that comes when lives are cut short, when family members are lost, and when those who are left behind must fill not only the newly created emotional chasms but also the gaps left in social and economic networks. Some communicated their sentiments with just an eloquent nod of the head rather than a story. That Thanksgiving season suffering was transformed into a communal experience of consolation undergirded by a profound sense of gratitude.

"The Lord Jesus on the night when he was betrayed took a loaf of bread, and when he had given thanks. . . . " What are we thankful for?

- That on the other side of the raging river someone is holding my baby
- That I have had no amputations
- That you are eating dinner in my house

- For hospitality
- For friends who are with us when we are in need
- For a pillar of light
- For the mountain of tortillas on the table every day
- That we are God's people

> ### Many Thanksgivings
>
> I'm grateful for all of the years of relationship with SMC beginning with the land legalization. This has allowed us to be here and to flourish. The funding for land apportionment gave some the opportunity who could not have afforded it.
>
> I am happy about the organization within our community. This started in Mesa Grande. We are not as well-organized now, but we are still organized. We are very excited about the partnership with the Ministry of Agriculture. Out of six projects that applied, the Valle Nuevo project was deemed the best. It is a good opportunity to bring the youth into the cooperative and give them training. The diversification of the economy brings us hope.
>
> *Pedro Membreño, Valle Nuevo*

Chapter 5

Sharing

> The Lord Jesus on the night when he was betrayed took a loaf of bread and when he had given thanks he broke it and said, "This is my body that is for you."
>
> 1 Corinthians 11:23–24

Margarita's new house and old

"We've been honored to have you as our guests at the camp meeting, and now you are about to head home to El Salvador," David Janzen addressed Tomasa Torres, Salomé Ascencio, and Margarita Avilez who sat in a circle

65

with representatives from the various Shalom Mission communities. The setting was the Gatlins' Waco living room, Monday, October 11, 2004. It was a rare occasion when a face-to-face meeting of those separated by the chasm was held in an SMC home rather than on a Valle Nuevo verandah. The three members of the Valle Nuevo *directiva* fortunately had been able to get visas from the United States government so they could travel to the states for the SMC biannual reunion.

Elsewhere in the Hope Fellowship neighborhood, some sixty additional members of the communities were wrapping up the weekend with workshops or just personal visits with friends from across the country before they would begin their respective journeys home. The theme for the weekend was "One New Humanity," brought into focus by the Apostle Paul's vision for reconciliation in Christ of two very diverse first century groups in the Roman empire, Jews and Gentiles: "He has abolished the law with its commandments and ordinances, that he might create in himself one new humanity in place of the two, thus making peace" (Eph 2:15). The invitation for the reunion contextualized the theme:

> Jesus has broken down the dividing wall of hostility. Church of the Sojourners, Hope Fellowship, Plow Creek Fellowship, Reba Place Fellowship, friends from Valle Nuevo in El Salvador, and other sister communities are coming together for three days to experience and celebrate the new culture of grace and reconciliation that has been created in God's people. Join us for the fun and the challenge.

On Saturday afternoon Nancy Gatlin had summoned all of the SMC attendees, "Tomasa, Margarita, and Salomé are your family. What do you do for family? You send them pictures, you phone them, you write them, you visit them. Consider visiting Valle Nuevo. They love to receive us and host us, to know that they are not forgotten." In conversations, addresses, meetings, and worship throughout the three days the affirmation of our friendship and family-hood had been encouraged and affirmed.

In the Gatlins' living room David continued, "For many years we have been in a relationship with your community." As Nancy translated, Tomasa, Salomé, and Margarita all nodded in turn. "When there are needs, friends share with friends and family members help each other. Is there any specific way we can help with your needs in Valle Nuevo?"

> ### Lasting Friendship
>
> Projects come and go, but the friendship with Shalom Mission Communities lasts.
>
> TOMASA TORRES, VALLE NUEVO

There was a pregnant pause in the room and some perceptible nervousness. In the early days of the relationship SMC had undertaken one major project with Valle Nuevo that involved the purchase of the agricultural land, but since that time financial assistance had been isolated and limited intentionally to small-scale needs. Everyone including the Valle Nuevo *directiva* knew that money or material aid flowing in only one direction could come to define the relationship and squeeze out the joy and love found in mutuality.

> ### The Purchase of the Land
>
> As we returned from our first delegation trip in 1992, we wondered how we could possibly convey to our people back home at Reba and Plow Creek and to our network of Overground Railroad friends what had happened in our visit and what God was doing that now included both us and Valle Nuevo. We would have to depend on God for that too.
>
> A few months later we received a message from the directiva saying that a large plot of land, about a square kilometer, had become available on El Picacho, the mountain adjacent to their community on the north side. If they could buy this steep mountain—and northern Cabañas is nothing but steep mountains—it would be enough, in good years, to grow the corn and beans they need to feed their families. That meant the men could stay home year-round, and the community could hope for some economic development. Without this land there was nothing else within walking distance, and their goal of self-sufficiency would be out of reach. The men would have to become migrants seeking seasonal labor in neighboring countries—as is the pattern in many destitute rural communities—just to feed their families. This is the wretched life they had before the war. To buy the land they would need $25,000 down and another $25,000 within a year. Could we help?

SECTION 2: PRACTICES OF A TRANSNATIONAL COMMUNION

> I took a few days of retreat in prayer at Plow Creek and asked God for a word. The time had come to close down the Overground Railroad because the Peace Accords in El Salvador had slowed the exodus of refugees who now had hope of security and peace back home. The network that had grown up caring for refugees had one last task, to secure a sanctuary for the village of Valle Nuevo. When I shared this plan at Reba, Plow Creek, and in the Overground Railroad network, there was assent. This is what God wants. Let's raise the $25,000 this year and trust that other groups will come together to raise the rest next year. And that is what happened.
>
> DAVID JANZEN, REBA PLACE FELLOWSHIP

In a transnational relationship between mission-oriented churches from the United States and Latin American communities impoverished by centuries of imperialism and war, there are many ways that the donation of material or financial aid can go wrong. It can create an unhealthy dependence, extend an economic arrangement that is foundationally unjust, cause divisions among recipients, assuage unexamined guilt for sin not yet acknowledged and confessed, and—most dangerous of all—perpetuate the misconception that sharing flows only in one direction.

During the reunion weekend in Waco, however, the SMC coordinators had gathered, prayed, and concluded it was unacceptable to hold onto the position that the relationship would not involve further financial involvement. The great chasm in Jesus's parable was a direct result of the nonresponse of the rich man to privilege and economic disparity. It was impossible to build a span across the chasm, to be in a relationship with each other, without addressing financial issues. When Jesus sat at the table with his disciples for his last supper, he said grace over the provision for that day, and then broke the bread, sharing it with his disciples, telling them, "This is my body that is for you." What is given for the common good, which is actually everything, should not be hoarded or tightly clenched. In the realm of God, in the spirit of Jesus who gave his life to his disciples, we likewise should give thanks and say, "this that I have is for you."

> ### The Great Collaboration
>
> A shortcoming of projects is they can easily categorize the participants into two classes, donors and beneficiaries, and then communion is lost. The fundamental collaboration in the gospel story is a relationship, not a project. It began in creation and took form when God established a people through Abraham and Sarah. The relationship matured in Jesus when he defeated the powers and principalities of selfishness, greed, ethnocentricity, gender bias, and violence through his suffering and death. And the relationship was fulfilled as the Holy Spirit worked through Paul, other apostles, and the believers to proliferate Jesus-communities in an expanding network across the world. SMC is part of this network. Our relationship with Valle Nuevo helps substantiate the reality of the collaboration. This historical community of communities is the great collaboration.
>
> JOE GATLIN, HOPE FELLOWSHIP

By that Monday morning the visitation had been underway for almost a week. Tomasa, Salomé, and Margarita had spent time prior to the weekend reunion getting to know the Waco area and other parts of the extended SMC family. Nancy had taken them to the World Hunger Relief, Inc., (WHRI) farm just outside of town where they spent an afternoon visiting with Neil Miller, the executive director who was also a Hope Fellowship member. Neil explained the farm's training programs and demonstration efforts and heard from the *directiva* members, particularly Salomé, about the challenges *campesinos* were facing in producing cash crops.

On Wednesday evening Hope Fellowship had hosted a conversation in its meeting house between the Salvadoran guests and Baylor University students studying economics as well as early SMC arrivals. Margarita opened the session with a reading of some of her poetry. Tomasa spoke next, telling their story of the flight across the Lempa, the years of exile in Honduras, and their return in 1989 when peace and the resolution of the civil war were being negotiated. Many of them had carried salvaged lumber from the refugee camp and with no tools built homes, piecing together ill-fitting boards and filling the cracks with mud. Since those earliest days, she explained, there had been many development efforts in their community.

Someone asked about Habitat for Humanity. A Habitat representative had been to the community in recent months, Tomasa responded, but the

Section 2: Practices of a Transnational Communion

Habitat model, which requires repayment, did not seem feasible due to the absence of any cash economy in Valle Nuevo.

Salomé then took the floor to share about their economic situation and how the free trade agreement with the United States (in English known as the Central American Free Trade Agreement, CAFTA) and government-subsidized imports had driven down the local price of corn. What had worked for generations would no longer produce income. The outlay to grow a bushel of corn had become greater than the revenue it produced.

Some university students from the economics department had a number of questions. Salomé carefully walked through all of his costs ending with a clear conclusion: it was impossible to make a living by growing corn. One student made the point that markets change and producers have to adjust and change, or . . . or. . . . The speaker did not want to finish his sentence when he realized he was about to repudiate Salomé's life. How was a *campesino* to adapt? The impossibility of the situation hung in silence before everyone in the room. A local economy had been destroyed. There were no easy answers.

Salomé cocked his head, smiled, extended his arms to either side, and held his hands open as though giving a blessing. He then said, simply and softly, without bitterness or rancor, "*Somos el cristo en la cruz del tratado de libre comercio*—We are the christ on the cross of free trade." The SMC members in the room could not help but recall Christ's command, to "take up the cross and follow me (Matt 10:38)."

> ### You are Welcome Here
>
> We have a saying about politicians—'A man caresses a horse to get on top of it!' But we don't believe you are here to exploit us. Yes, during the war, your country brought mines, ideologies and people against us. But we respect you for opening the subject. Your religion serves to build family . . . whether you come with assistance or not, you are welcome here.
>
> Miguel Parapeto, Valle Nuevo

The trail of suffering does not go far before it forks. The obvious and easy branch is self-pity; it leads downward with no resistance through resentment, isolation, and bitterness to a dark and desolate dead-end. The other option—as though it is hidden beneath dense overgrowth—is more difficult to find. It is noticed by only those travelers who are stooped by the weight of a submissive spirit. Those who take the obscure path—the narrow way is what Jesus called it (Matt 7:14)—discover two things as they struggle to climb a serious grade: one, long-suffering is truly long; and two, God provides angels for the journey, compassionate human beings who walk alongside in a spirit of accompaniment.

> ### They Won't Let Me Carry Water
>
> When I let people know at home why I was coming, they wanted to hear what I was going to do for these people. What has happened to me here is to see that I am a rather helpless and useless person here. We have heard that 'power corrupts' and I'm beginning to see that this has happened to all of us. I've had an attitude that because I'm an American, I know what others need and can help them. But being here is pretty humbling. I can't speak their language. They won't let me carry water. I need all kinds of special help.
>
> DAVID FITZ, A FRIEND OF SMC

When there are needs, friends share with friends and family members help each other. Of course. As kin, how can we keep from helping? In a family people give and share of whatever resource they have whether material, emotional, spiritual, or even time. When a basic need is unmet everything else is dropped and the counting of cost becomes secondary. Ruth Anne Friesen of Reba Place in Evanston can testify to this truth.

> ### Sharing Friendship
>
> We were at Angelina and Pedro's house as dusk deepened into evening. Angelina had made pupusas for dinner, including some with the *loroco* vine flower. As we sat drinking sweet coffee, a storm that had been gathering burst open over us. A young woman with bright eyes asked where I had learned Spanish and eagerly offered to show me her English homework. She showed me to her front room while she dug around in her bedroom to find her notebook. She excitedly showed me her soccer jersey that advocated scoring goals to fight violence against women, which she spoke passionately about. We sat down and began reviewing English words and pronunciation (which she was very good at).

Section 2: Practices of a Transnational Communion

> She told me she had recently gone back to finish high school after an attempt to emigrate to the U.S. had left her lost in the desert for three days. As the rain pounded down in the dark around us, kids and adults gathered together, some settling in to old familiar friendships and others creating new ones for the first time.
>
> *Sage Johnson, Church of the Sojourners*

In 2012 Ruth Anne returned to Central America where she and her beloved husband Richard, who passed away in 2010, served in the mid-nineties with the Mennonite Central Committee. After visiting with friends in Colombia she traveled on to El Salvador to join the SMC delegation, arriving a few days early so she would have extra time to visit with some of the brothers and sisters in Valle Nuevo whom she had known for years.

Friday morning, while sitting on the verandah of Rosa's and Pastor's house, she cut a piece of garlic with her pocketknife and, as is her practice to help ward off intestinal troubles, swallowed it whole. The swallow, though, was not as big as the garlic which lodged in her esophagus and began to burn her throat.

Coughing would not make it come up; swallowing would not make it go down. Ruth Anne, choking for breath and with tears in her eyes, appeared on the verandah and managed to make herself understood. Rosa flew down the hill, around the soccer field, past the chapel to the medical clinic and brought back a nurse. By the time they arrived, Ruth Anne was able to breathe, but the garlic had staked its claim, it was not going to move.

Word spreads magically when there is a health crisis and within a few minutes one of the neighbor's sons arrived with a pickup. Ruth Anne turned to Rosa and managed to gasp a breathless request, "Please stay with me."

It was no small matter for Rosa to leave her home. Like most of the other women of Valle Nuevo Rosa is always carrying something, a grandbaby on her hip, a tub of tortillas in her hands, a bundle of firewood under her arms. Managing the economy of her *campesino* household, she supervises the kitchen, provides hospitality to expected and unexpected guests, sees the children off to school, takes care of the chickens, elderly parents, and the destitute of the community who may drop in at any moment, and manages the storage of the water since it flows through the pipes only one or maybe two days a month.

Sharing

But there was no hesitation on Rosa's part. Ruth Anne was in need. "Ask and it will be given you," Jesus had told his disciples (Matt 7:7). Both asking and giving are necessary for a community's healthy economy. Rosa grabbed Ruth Anne with one hand and a pail with the other to catch the steady stream of saliva Ruth Anne was producing as they jumped in the truck for the forty-five-minute drive to Sensuntepeque, the largest city in Cabañas.

Twelve hours, an ambulance ride, and two hospitals later in the capital city of San Salvador, the intractable chunk of garlic finally surrendered to a doctor who had the right equipment. All along the way Rosa had held Ruth Anne's hand, balanced the pail on her knee, and made calls with her cell phone tucked under her chin. There was no time to eat and no time to rest.

Late that evening Dawn, Nancy, and Joe arrived in San Salvador for the delegation and made their way to the hospital. They wandered through the dark hallways looking for Ruth Anne and party. "Go this way," one nurse said. "Go that way," a nun said. Eventually it was a bone-weary Rosa who found them and led them through the labyrinth of corridors to a simple, spartan recovery room. There Ruth Anne, freed from the squatter that had inflamed her throat and tormented her all day, sat straight up in her bed, smiling radiantly.

Ruth Anne would later explain, "When I woke up from surgery there were many who had gathered and the realization struck, all were great sisters and brothers whom I very much needed and was so glad to see, Rosalinda, Mercedes, and Susana, Nancy and Joe, and Dawn. Folks who clearly represented God's love surrounded me. Rosa had cared all the way with only a bottle of Gatorade to sustain her. She had been a very faithful friend! Going through a difficult time knits people together."

To say that Rosa merely accompanied Ruth Anne on her trip does not begin to describe the encouragement, hope, and spiritual support her presence lent to Ruth Anne throughout that trying day. In English an accompaniment is typically something that supplements or complements but is, in essence, ornamental and unnecessary, maybe even incidental. *Acompañamiento* in Spanish is much more substantial; *acompañamiento* occurs when one walks or travels with another through hardship. On that difficult day in 2012 Rosa was a companion and a comrade, a friend and a co-laborer.

> ### A Glimpse of the Gospel
>
> The relationship with Valle Nuevo, El Salvador, has been formative in my life. Pastor's and Rosa's porch with its cleanly-swept tiles, chickens running between legs, and promise of good company has reminded me that the Church has no borders. I believe this connection with Valle Nuevo gives each of our communities a fuller glimpse of the gospel.
>
> ANALÍ GATLIN LOOPER, HOPE FELLOWSHIP

Back in the Waco living room on that Monday morning in the fall of 2004, the SMC coordinators wondered if their twelve years of *acompañamiento* legitimized their explicit offer of open-handed, assistance, "Is there any specific way we can help with your needs in Valle Nuevo?" Would the help be perceived as the left-overs from the wealthy *patron's* table? Would the *campesinos* feel diminished by the *gringos*?

The *directiva* members, Tomasa, Margarita, and Salomé, exchanged glances and silently communicated with each other, referencing strategies they previously had discussed. Would they make the right request, they wondered. Were they about to ask too much?

Tomasa gave a slight nod to Salomé; he would serve as the initial spokesman.

Salomé sat silent for a long minute, then cocked his head, smiled, and carefully and distinctly with guileless dignity, said "We still have ten families who live in houses made with the lumber they brought back in 1989 from the Honduran refugee camp. These families cannot afford to build decent homes. We can use your help." That his family was one of the ten caused him no hesitation, embarrassment, or shame. "Ask and it shall be given."

The SMC people in the room gave a sigh of relief. Their offer had been accepted with a very specific response. SMC and Valle Nuevo each had anticipated the readiness of the other.

The two groups in the room quickly became one planning team and confirmed the agreement of the Holy Spirit. They invoked and welcomed God's partnership in the proposed venture for it was very large and complicated. Nancy continued to translate as various concerns and considerations emerged and details took form. The approximate cost would be fifty thousand dollars, funds that were not on hand and a sum that was sizable for the four Shalom Mission communities. The coordinators agreed they would need to check back with their respective communities about taking on this financial challenge.

Conversation moved to challenges even greater than raising funds. Tomasa told the SMC coordinators they could not just send money for such a large sum would tear their community apart. Salomé added that they would not know how to manage a project like this. Moreover, although the government had agreed to land reform so the *campesinos* would be able to take ownership of land they had worked for generations as indentured servants, there had been no progress after years of working on title problems for both agricultural and residential property.

Despite these issues the *directiva* members and the coordinators wrapped up the meeting with confidence. For the first time since the commitment by Plow Creek and Reba Place a decade earlier to help with land purchase, the communities would undertake a large, development project.

Before the *campesinos* left Waco, they had one more conversation with Neil to let him know they were interested in developing a partnership with World Hunger Relief. WHRI, which had been looking for some time to expand its international programs beyond a long-standing relationship with an effort in Haiti, had developed a set of criteria for ideal partnerships. Tomasa, Salomé, Margarita, and Neil, after discussion about the respective assets of Valle Nuevo and WHRI, concluded that a partnership would be a good fit. They agreed to pray about the possibility of developing some exchanges.

WHRI and Valle Nuevo

World Hunger Relief, Inc., made a strategic decision in the mid-two thousands to develop partnerships with local organizations in developing countries. At about the same time the SMC retreat was hosted in Waco and three members of the *directiva* were able to attend, our International Programs committee developed a set of criteria for ideal partnerships and prayed that God would bring these plans to fruition.

For various reasons, our good intentions didn't begin to bear fruit until the fall of 2009. I made plans to make World Hunger's first visit to the community together with my daughter Emily who previously had been part of an SMC delegation. I remember well making this plan known at an SMC gathering and receiving, to my surprise, a hearty round of applause. It was clear that our reaching out to the Valle Nuevo community was an initiative not only of World Hunger, but that

> we were also furthering the mission of SMC. The significance of this support was enormous as it allowed us to walk into the community having inherited the trust of a more than twenty-year relationship.
>
> Another remarkable confirmation of the rightness of this initiative came as we were preparing to make our first visit to Valle Nuevo. Emily, and I were visiting Mark Menjivar, a documentary photographer from San Antonio, married to a former WHRI intern. As I shared with Mark our plans to begin working in El Salvador, I watched incredulity creep into his face. "Did you know that my father is Salvadoran, and that I lived there as a child?" he asked me. "And did you know I've been looking for an excuse to go back?" Mark went with us on that trip and returned three more times to document the struggle and hope of the Valle Nuevo community. *Retorno*, his photo-documentary told the moving story of the community's return to Santa Marta, their young people's return from university studies, and Mark's return to the land of his father.
>
> Our mandate from the directiva was twofold: 1) learn and tell their stories and 2) help develop economic opportunities that could keep their young people employed after university studies. We initially worked alongside a group of Santa Marta youth to promote vegetable production, an enterprise that seemed profitable, and an attractive alternative to the traditional corn and beans grown in the milpa. They were interested in moving from high-input hydroponics to organic production, and we helped them take the initial steps in developing this approach.
>
> We soon discovered, however, that the Valle Nuevo *directiva* had a separate history and identity which eventually resulted in a parallel initiative. Our relationship with Valle Nuevo shifted away from agricultural support and toward exchanges in which World Hunger interns lived among the community to serve and learn alongside them.
>
> NEIL ROWE MILLER,
> FORMER EXECUTIVE DIRECTOR OF WORLD HUNGER RELIEF
> AND MEMBER OF HOPE FELLOWSHIP

By the close of 2004, the SMC communities were gathering funds for the housing project, some through inheritances that community members had received. The issues of financial, construction, and overall project management, however, remained unsolved.

In February 2005, Joe, who worked for Habitat for Humanity International, attended a conference in Honduras and by providence was assigned Carlos Avalos, the Church Relations Director for El Salvador Habitat, as his roommate. As is common for strangers thrown into a relationship by a conference they began to look for common experiences. Joe shared with Carlos about his recent visit at Christmas in El Salvador.

"Where were you?" Carlos asked.

"A tiny community called Valle Nuevo, part of the larger village of Santa Marta, in the northern part of the country."

"No way!" Carlos said. "I know Valle Nuevo." It turned out not only was he the Habitat representative who Tomasa reported had made a visit to their community, he also had been part of the youth group that welcomed the people of Valle Nuevo at the border with songs when they returned from exile in 1989. Joe explained to Carlos the obstacles Shalom Missions faced in helping to address Valle Nuevo housing issues.

Carlos mused, "I think El Salvador Habitat can help."

"No way," Joe responded, thinking about Habitat's repayment requirement. "You don't understand. These people cannot afford a Habitat house."

"Oh, I do understand. I was there," Carlos said. "With your involvement, I think we can be creative."

It was a loaves and fishes story. By the end of the year Shalom Missions had raised the money and Habitat for Humanity of El Salvador had fine-tuned and readied its model that would include various levels of subsidy determined by the income of the different homeowners. The deepest subsidies would be covered by a designated gift from a specific donor, namely Shalom Missions. Waco Habitat for Humanity soon joined in the effort by designating its "tithe money" (ten percent of its funds raised in Waco) for the project.

Throughout 2006, Habitat worked with the Valle Nuevo *directiva* in preparing for the management and administration of the building project and with individual families through a socio-economic assessment and readiness program. The partnership proceeded apace through 2007 and 2008. The Valle Nuevo *directiva* claimed it had never worked with an outside development organization like El Salvador Habitat that did what it said it would do, when it said it would do it, and the Habitat leadership, for its part, said it had never worked with a rural community that had so much leadership and was so self-organized.

Section 2: Practices of a Transnational Communion

On October 29th, 2008, the nineteenth anniversary of the community's return from Honduras, Valle Nuevo held a huge fiesta. Fernando Arroyo and Joe representing Shalom Missions and John Alexander representing Waco Habitat for Humanity (all three from Hope Fellowship) were able to attend and join the festivities. The day was marked by a special mass, a *pupusa* eating contest, foot races around the square for both men and women, and the dedication of not just ten but twenty Habitat houses funded by Shalom Mission Communities and Waco Habitat. For the first time this day of repatriation was celebrated with an event equal in scope to the annual March commemoration of the Lempa massacre.

With its toe-hold in Valle Nuevo, El Salvador Habitat also began work for the first time in the larger community of Santa Marta. By the summer of 2009, fifty Habitat houses were completed in Valle Nuevo and Santa Marta. Within the next couple of years El Salvador Habitat would add another ten homes and by 2017 a total of sixty-three families in the community were living in Habitat for Humanity homes with another ten planned later in the year.

Since that meeting in 2004, there has been a steady growth in development activity in Valle Nuevo. Habitat for Humanity continues to work with Valle Nuevo and Santa Marta, World Hunger Relief has helped implement several projects and had two interns live for extended times in the community, the agricultural cooperative was reborn, and a water project as well as a transnational collaboration to develop and fund micro-enterprises were launched.

Excerpts from Valle Nuevo Youth Group business plan for egg production, April 2015

After the peace agreements were signed, the first group from Shalom Missions arrived to offer a gesture of solidarity to our community. Through this relationship, we have had the opportunity to create a partnership between World Hunger Relief and the community of Valle Nuevo.

Expectations:

- To produce jobs for the group and all persons in the group
- To create a training program for the youth
- To generate employment
- To see more development in the community

Sharing

> *Spiritual component*:
>
> We are created by God as people with dignity who have been given strength to earn our daily bread and to be able to work together as brothers and sisters within the group and the community.
>
> We wish to begin a project that will benefit the inhabitants of our community, assisting them in obtaining local resources for a dignified life.

Development in Santa Marta, however, is neither the formal purpose nor the planned destination of the Shalom Missions-Valle Nuevo association. Development has not been our strategy for achieving justice or absolving guilt. Development activity instead is a form of sharing; it is the natural outgrowth of a relationship in which two communities and their individual members have accompanied each other in suffering and thanksgiving.

We may enjoy what we have earned, we may be pleased with the recompense received for our labor, and we may be proud when our merit is acknowledged and awarded, but genuine gratitude is reserved for gifts. And gifts from God are meant to be shared. "Freely you have received, freely give," Jesus told his disciples (Matt 10:8, NIV).

Ruth Anne after her 2012 visit explained the spirit of our sharing this way,

> It was a treasure to hear from Tomasa and Morena at supper about how the love of God is infinite, gifted, and shared as we walk together over time! The love is given as if we are family sharing life and fellowship together over meals. It is the grace of God pouring out love that can never be repaid from either side! Tomasa noted that we are all invited to work together in the vineyard, and we are all paid the same no matter how long we have worked. We are brothers and sisters and part of the family of God as we together do the will of God.

> ### From the Heart
>
> It is a relationship from the heart between our communities.
>
> *Juana Lainez, Valle Nuevo*

Section 2: Practices of a Transnational Communion

Eventually the narrow way, the path of suffering, empties into a clearing, and in the light of joy the pilgrims can see that all good things, the things for which we are most deeply grateful—a loaf of bread, a mountain of tortillas, and a community of new homes—are gifts from a loving God.

Chapter 6

Remembering

"Do this in remembrance of me." In the same way he took the cup also, after supper, saying, "This cup is the new covenant in my blood. Do this, as often as you drink it, in remembrance of me."

1 Corinthians 11:24c–25

The Monument to Truth and Memory

Section 2: Practices of a Transnational Communion

The Monument to Truth and Memory stands as a permanent feature of the landscape, unchanging and immovable, buttressing a hillside in an urban park in San Salvador. It endures in the minds of the visitors who walk its length as a visual image, not so much because of its imposing size and quiet elegance but because its impact is engraved on the moral conscience. The names of thirty thousand individuals who were killed or disappeared during the civil war of the eighties are etched in white on its endless death row of black, granite panels. And this is only a partial record of the brutality. Including military, more than 70,000 people lost their lives in the conflict. The weight of this memory would be crushing if it was not borne by all of us, young and old, civilians and soldiers, victims and executioners, Salvadorans and United States visitors, *campesinos* and SMC delegates.

The emotional impact of a visit to the wall on Sunday afternoon, the first full day of the annual SMC delegation visit, lingers with the delegates and often colors the informal conversations that take place later that day on the back patio of El Torogoz Hotel, a guest house in San Salvador. Twilight quickly brushes away the heat and humidity of a June afternoon, and an evening on the patio with the gracious hospitality of the Torogoz staff offers a superb opportunity to catch up on friendships, to meet some new folks from other communities, and just to debrief from the day.

> ### The Memorial Wall
>
> The memorial wall was sad but powerful. It was very stressful to be at the wall. What comes to mind is that the memorial wall is for the people of El Salvador because it carries the memory of the tragedies that happened there. It is not for the soldiers and the military and death squads, although they need to remember, too. It makes me think how can we break the cycles of oppression and war.
>
> Megan Herring, Reba Place Fellowship

"Adam, how do you keep alive the memory of Valle Nuevo back at home?" Joe asked. Adam Vaughn is from Reba Place and was on his second visit as a delegate. No matter if it is a first or fifteenth visit, the initial twenty-four hours in El Salvador provide abundant sights and impressions, and a time to muse and converse is welcomed.

It had been a long day. That morning after their arrival on Saturday evening the delegation traveled downtown to the National Cathedral and attended the "popular" mass, or the mass of the people, replete with guitars, lay leadership, and a homily of hope for justice and liberation. Afterwards the delegates walked through the city's central plaza where in 1980 thousands of Salvadorans attending Archbishop Romero's funeral were fired upon by government troops. They then traced the two-block flight of the mourners who were seeking refuge to the Cathedral El Rosario, an edifice that from the outside looks like a concrete bunker or funeral vault, but whose interior is a paradise ethereally lit through multi-colored stained glass windows. In the afternoon, the delegates walked the wall of Truth and Memory, where there are only a few places to escape the hot afternoon sun, and then returned to El Torogoz to relax for the balance of the afternoon. Later that evening about thirty students from Valle Nuevo and Santa Marta who are attending university in the capital city would arrive at the guest house for a dinner hosted by the SMC delegates.

> ### The Stations of the Cross
>
> At each station, the suffering of Jesus paralleled a point where the people suffered in their flight to Honduras. Ending at the church, several hundred people listened to the priest read the names of relatives who died in the war and the crossing.
>
> DAVID HOVDE, REBA PLACE FELLOWSHIP

"Do we have to remember?" the emotions protest. The memories are painful. Forgetting looks attractive when remembering triggers grief over the premature loss of seventy thousand human lives. But remembering is unavoidable because it is the design. The death brought by the war should not be forgotten; it cannot be forgotten. Archbishop Romero and his proclamation of hope, the flight to the Lempa, suffering in the refugee camps, and disappearance and death must all be remembered. Through corporate remembering our historical and current communities find solidarity.

They Help Us Remember

These internationals come to us, and they value all that we are doing even more than we value it ourselves. In their eyes what we have done is significant. There are five communities and hundreds of people who will hear their report. They help us remember why we are a community and what we struggle for.

Tomasa Torres, Valle Nuevo

Being remembered was important even to Jesus, maybe especially to Jesus. "Do this in remembrance" is the one command found in the institution passage.

Memory is paramount. Animals may be able to live without it and survive by instinct, but we as human beings need to be both the rememberer and the remembered. At every turn along the way of life as well as on the non-ending straightaway that proclaims death, remembering is essential to know who we are. And to not be remembered . . . is simply to not be. With no memorial or tombstone, the faces and names of those who have left are wiped clean from the surface of the earth, and their legacy of spirit and hope is lost.

Remembering Is Not Just a God Story . . .

Scripture is filled with the admonition to remember, to remember on purpose, to remember so as not to forget. Part of what went wrong for the Israelites in the land of milk and honey was that they did not remember, as they were told to, that they too were slaves in Egypt. . . .

They were called to celebrate the Passover, a meal filled with memory joggers like bitter herbs, unleavened bread, and a roasted lamb. Remembering. Not just with our heads, but with our mouths and bellies, our heart and gut. . . .

Its not just a God story; it's a 'we' story; it's a story of God encountering his people and his people encountering God. . . .

Remembering is much of what the church must do in order to live a faithful life. Remembering is at the heart of the Eucharist, the keeping of Sabbath, of Advent and Christmas, of Lent and Easter. Much of all our eating together centers on remembering.

Debbie Gish, Church of the Sojourners

Remembering also bridges the chasms that separate contemporaries. Re-member: to reunite that which was joined. The hope of the gospel in Jesus Christ is that the fractured parts of God's creation will be brought together and re-membered in the new creation. The divisions caused by sin, greed, and domination that date back through the centuries will give way to an even more ancient truth and memory of our fellowship with the divine and our community with each other.

> **Please Remember Us!**
>
> Their desire for relationship, to not be forgotten, came through in every conversation.
>
> DAVID JANZEN, REBA PLACE FELLOWSHIP

"Please don't forget us!" members of the Valle Nuevo community have regularly shared this earnest plea with their visitors from the United States. In earlier years this supplication was accentuated with the gravity of an official farewell when one of the members of the *directiva*, most often Pastor, would stand at the close of the *despedida* and give it earnest voice, "What we want more than anything is for you not to forget us. Please remember us!" It was as though, at the moment the delegates prepared to leave, the chasm yawned larger and deeper, pernicious and miasmic, gobbling land at the edge of the village, threatening to consume Valle Nuevo's identity if not the community itself.

We all want to be remembered. Many of the SMC delegates have been moved when they return and find pictures of themselves from previous delegations on the walls of Valle Nuevo homes or on the last and most recent page of the thin photo albums of family pictures kept by many of the Valle Nuevo hosts. When we see evidence that we are remembered, all of us are quickened in our spirits and become more deeply aware of our shared humanity.

Across distance and through time remembering requires ceaseless initiative and conscious effort. The annual SMC visit to Valle Nuevo is itself an act of remembering. The delegates go to create new or regenerate existing connections and in doing so make new memories that are then kept alive through telling stories, giving thanks, and the sharing of life in successive delegations.

Section 2: Practices of a Transnational Communion

> **From the Information Sheet Sent to Delegates Each Year**
>
> What is a delegation?
>
> The SMC delegation is not a traditional mission trip nor an exposure trip. Our home communities have "delegated" us to visit the community of Valle Nuevo and continue building upon this long-standing relationship. Over the twenty plus years of our relationship with Valle Nuevo, SMC has participated in projects to help secure individual and communal land titles, has facilitated the initial work of Habitat El Salvador in Valle Nuevo as well as the initial work of the World Hunger Relief's sustainable agricultural projects. However, the primary purpose of the delegation is to visit with our friends in Valle Nuevo.
>
> Come on the delegation anticipating the opportunity to build relationship with our "*compañero/as*" in Valle Nuevo and the youth who live in Santa Marta (the town in which Valle Nuevo is located) as well as those who study at the university in San Salvador. This delegation is also a good opportunity for building friendships among us from SMC.
>
> Some of you will be visiting Valle Nuevo for the first time, and others of us will be returning. Each of us may travel with particular goals, but we all represent the Shalom Missions Communities on this delegation. Ask your sending community what hopes they have for your participation in the delegation. What would they like you to report on when you return?
>
> The SMC delegation is also an act of community. We represent a community association and we travel as a community. It can be awkward at times to travel as foreigners in a large group, but we ask that you come on the delegation prepared to participate in all scheduled activities unless you are sick.

"How do you keep the memory of Valle Nuevo alive back at home?" It was a legitimate question and opened the type of conversation delegates expect to have with each other in their first three days in the capital city. That much time before traveling to Valle Nuevo—when the whole trip is only nine days—may seem excessive, but it provides an accessible entrance into Salvadoran culture and history and an opportunity for community-building with the delegate team. By the time the coaster bus heads for Valle Nuevo on Tuesday, the eight to fifteen delegates are a functional family with an understanding of who speaks Spanish well, who is an extrovert and who is an introvert, who can help lift spirits, who can establish a theological framework for the experience at hand, who knows first aid, who can sing, who is a poet, who is hesitant about culinary adventures, who is a wanderer, and who will tether the wanderer.

Back at home Adam had become involved in SMC's Valle Nuevo Collaboration, an effort to promote and assist in the development of Valle Nuevo microenterprises and help broker their funding. Joe also knew that Adam, with this being his second delegation, was aware that memory would be an important theme throughout the visit.

"Well . . . " Adam drew the word out, buying some time. He closed his eyes for a second, trying to remember how he would go about remembering Valle Nuevo. "Well . . . " he repeated, "life just gets really busy with three young children and everything else. I don't have a ton of time to just sit around and think." Everything else for Adam includes a host of responsibilities that he and his wife Stephanie carry for Reba Place Fellowship and Reba Place Church as well as providing leadership for two community-run businesses, Plain and Simple, a furniture store with Amish designs, and a new home-care services for seniors. Joe waited patiently and expectantly, his arms folded in front of him on the patio table; he wasn't going to let Adam off the hook.

Adam smiled and then continued by talking about the artwork on the walls in the Vaughan home and the four mosaic tiles commemorating Valle Nuevo history that were made by children during one of the SMC reunions and now hang in the Reba Place meeting house. He also shared that he would regularly read the blog post of Eli Ross, an intern from the World Hunger Relief farm in Waco who spent a year in Valle Nuevo. He mentioned the occasional news updates from Valle Nuevo that David Janzen, a member of Adam's small group at Reba, would give. He talked about a recent evening when their small group looked up facts together about El Salvador on the internet. While they ate *pupusas*, the adults regaled the children with stories of meals and visits in Valle Nuevo.

SECTION 2: PRACTICES OF A TRANSNATIONAL COMMUNION

> ### The Hope Fellowship Spring Commemoration
>
> The March 18 Valle Nuevo Commemoration event was very meaningful to me. Having never been there, I find that I often feel disconnected from the relationship we as a church have with the people of Valle Nuevo. At the event, I gained new insights and understanding into the stories of their community.
>
> In particular, the unique focus at each stop on our walk helped me better understand the particularities of the needs, struggles, and triumphs of those living the Valle Nuevo. The stories were articulated well, from the land rights, the challenges the young people face, and the spiritual formation happening in the community.
>
> We were not intending to attend the event but ended up going because our older daughter wanted to after she heard Nancy Gatlin share the story of what it might have been like on the night our brothers and sisters had to flee and cross the Lempa River.
>
> In my mind, I have a picture of what Valle Nuevo is like, and I have imagined the faces of people living there. I hope to some day go myself and hear the stories firsthand, and meet my brothers and sisters face-to-face.
>
> KELLY LAWSON, HOPE FELLOWSHIP

The table provides a perfect setting for telling a story. Our memory is often not just of the story that was told, but rather of the telling of the story, the animation of the story-teller, possibly the visual setting of a meal at which it was told, and the company of those sitting around the table. Witness how many of the disciples' stories of their time with Jesus recorded in the gospel accounts had to do with meals.

On his last evening at the table with his disciples as they took the Passover meal, Jesus assigned the responsibility for memory to the very elemental act of dining together. Every time the disciples ate together they were, according to Jesus, to do so in his memory. The meal itself was to become the telling of a story, recalling when the Lord had physically walked, talked, camped out, and supped with the disciples. Breaking bread, sharing the cup, passing the platter of tortillas is the enactment of a drama that reinforces all that Jesus taught, modeled, and promised. Communion remembers Jesus and his disciples.

Remembering

The people of Valle Nuevo and Shalom Mission Communities have not always been able to sit at the table together. At one recent meal in Valle Nuevo there were knowing smiles around the table when Nancy recalled this fact. As servants, the *campesinos* served their overlords for generations, making sure their plates were full and then standing patiently to the side while the *patrones* ate. Only later would they eat, creating a dining form of apartheid. The people of Valle Nuevo brought this practice into the relationship with Shalom Missions, an uncomfortable custom for the delegates from the States.

> ## Food and Table Fellowship
> **From the General Information Document for Valle Nuevo-SMC Delegates**
>
> Quickly skim last year's schedule, and you'll notice that eating is one of our principal activities in El Salvador. Table fellowship is an important component of our time together as delegates and with our friends in Valle Nuevo. Some of our friends in Valle Nuevo will choose to sit with us when we eat, and others will refrain from eating with us as a sign of respect given to guests. Regardless of whether or not our hosts eat with us, they demonstrate their care for us by the provision of food on the table.
>
> We ask delegates to be willing to participate in table fellowship. There will be times when you may not be able to eat everything that is served, but you should be prepared to eat on a daily basis corn tortillas, beans, eggs, cheese, and fried plantains. If you have food concerns, please discuss them openly with the delegation leaders before making a decision to participate in the delegation. If you struggle with life threatening allergies or food sensitivities, participating in a delegation may not be the best way for you to engage in the SMC/Valle Nuevo relationship.

There have been adjustments on both sides. After a number of invitations to the table, boldness on the part of one group and patience on the part of the other, the taboo has been broken for many; northerners and southerners, men and women, children and aged can enjoy table fellowship together. There are still some of the *campesinos* who are hesitant, and, as is noted in the general information document given to delegation members, that is O.K. We are reminded that we continue to proclaim Christ's death until he comes again.

Adam paused, and then Joe prodded him again. "I know you love *pupusas*, Adam, but really, why are you back for another delegation? The itinerary is pretty much the same as it was two years ago." And Joe was right. There is not a lot of variety from one year to the next.

On Monday, after mass and the wall on Sunday, the delegates visit several sites related to the lives and assassinations of Archbishop Romero, the Jesuit priests at the UCA, and other martyrs. They also tour Fernando Llort's art gallery, El Arbol de Dios, and then visit with the artist and his family.

> ### The Art of Fernando Llort
>
> Fernando Llort was born in El Salvador in 1949. He originally studied for the priesthood in Colombia, France, and Belgium, but when he moved to the Salvadoran village of La Palma in 1972, he discovered his calling in art. Through art he reconnected with his Latin American roots and sought to "define our people in their human and spiritual dimensions."
>
> In La Palma Llort began to stylize the flowers, fields, birds, and animals familiar to all Salvadorans while retrieving Mayan and other pre-Columbian motifs. He opened workshops for people with no training in art to provide skills and employment. La Palma, now the country's best-known folk art center, has about 120 workshops producing cups, plates, potholders, boxes, crosses, and other objects for daily use.
>
> Llort's work includes paintings, prints, engravings, silk screens, lithographs, and handcrafted items. Religious symbols appear, such as hands upraised in worship, birds representing creation, and the sun as God's creative power. The designs and bright colors of not a few paintings celebrate the harmony of the universe and unity of humankind.
>
> Despite the devastation and suffering brought by El Salvador's civil war, Llort's art, paradoxically, visualized the cheerful, healthy, productive life as the true potential of the common people's existence. He has been widely recognized for affirming their identity. His larger works beautify many notable public and religious places.
>
> THOMAS FINGER, REBA PLACE CHURCH

On Tuesday, the delegates head to Valle Nuevo where that afternoon they will walk and view the tilapia ponds, the agricultural projects, the school, the children's center, the clinic, and then be welcomed at supper by the *directiva*. On Wednesday, they will visit with a number of individuals, maybe Tomasa, Margarita, Juana, or Felipa and Salomé, and in the afternoon they are likely to meet with some of the youth. That evening they will dine at someone else's house, probably on *pupusas*.

Thursday will feature the trip to the Lempa River, lunch at a restaurant in Sensuntepeque, and a stop at Radio Victoria, a community-run radio station with its roots in the resistance movement during the civil war. On Friday, there will likely be a community meeting at the communal house followed by the *despedida* with the *directiva* in the evening. On Saturday, the delegation will return to El Salvador, do a bit of souvenir shopping, and then eat dinner and pack for the early Sunday morning departure to their respective homes.

"Some would say, been there, done that," Joe continued and then pointed out—as if Adam didn't already know this—his absence for ten days had to be difficult for Stephanie who was back home with three young children. There were other challenges for Adam in making this trip again. He was responsible for two community businesses. His conversational Spanish was improving, but he still would need regular translation for the four days of meetings and visits in Valle Nuevo. And, given that Reba Place operates out of a common purse, the decision for Adam to go would have involved multiple parties and would not have been as simple as answering the question, "Do I have money in the bank or not for a trip like this?"

"So why are you back?"

Adam lifted a bemused eyebrow; he could have responded, "Why pick on me?" Six of the other seven participants in the 2015 delegation were returnees. Diamante Maya of Hope Fellowship was also a sophomore delegate. Fernando Arroyo of Hope Fellowship was on his third visit, Carol Youngquist of Reba Place her fourth, Dawn her eighth, and Joe his thirteenth.

How do you answer a "why" question like this? How can you describe the voice of the Lord? How can you explain the wall of truth and memory in your soul that clearly marks a path with this certain stop along the way? Always unfailingly polite and an ever-willing good sport, Adam gave it a try.

Sure, he liked to travel. Yes, he was interested in economic development and micro-enterprise. And, of course, getting away was difficult. That year, 2015, other Reba Fellowship people were not able to come, and a number of Fellowship folks were encouraging Adam to go again. The Reba Church World Missions committee paid the $550 delegation fee, points

SECTION 2: PRACTICES OF A TRANSNATIONAL COMMUNION

from a credit card used by the furniture business covered his airfare, and the Janzens were able to cover some other expenses with inheritance funds. There were challenges, but bottom line he could go when others for a variety of reasons could not. Plus, with the Valle Nuevo Collaboration, Adam had found a way to be involved on an ongoing basis.

> ### Why I Went on a Second Delegation
>
> In 2015 I was presented with the opportunity to return to El Salvador with the annual delegation. I went with low expectations. I wasn't sure if my presence would make much of a difference. And God proved me wrong. The people of El Salvador exude a deep appreciation for the visitors from our communities. I'm certain they would visit us if they could. However, in general, there's a lot more to overcome for them to be able to visit us. They are quite dependent on us visiting them. I heard it said more than once that they so much appreciate that we are not a project to them. We are brothers and sisters in Christ.
>
> One of our guiding Scriptures this year was Matthew 12:46–50: While Jesus was still talking to the crowd, his mother and brothers stood outside, wanting to speak to him. Someone told him, "Your mother and brothers are standing outside, wanting to speak to you." He replied to him, "Who is my mother, and who are my brothers?" Pointing to his disciples, he said, "Here are my mother and my brothers. For whoever does the will of my Father in heaven is my brother and sister and mother."
>
> My eyes have been opened to what a unique gift God has given us that for twenty-three years we have been able to sustain this relationship in which genuine mutual love is shared across borders, cultures, languages, and economic status. I had underestimated the power of presence even in such a short time. God met me very personally in His unique way and I realized what a gift I have been given to be "grandfathered" into this deep, rich, long-lasting relationship.
>
> DIAMANTE MAYA, HOPE FELLOWSHIP

As an aside, Adam noted, pausing in reflecting on his own motivations and connection, he was not alone in finding ways to make connections and contributions. Earlier that day, Diamante, sharing her confusion about who was who in the extended families of the *directiva* members, had offered to develop a Valle Nuevo family tree that could be used back in the Shalom Mission communities. Carol, who on her most recent trip had heard interest from some in Valle Nuevo about learning how to knit, brought knitting supplies.

Adam finally arrived at his most compelling reason for returning, "There are many who have gone before and devoted their heart and soul to this relationship." He recounted the story he knew very well of David Janzen's walk and conversation with Yvonne Dilling almost twenty-five years earlier. And then he reflected, "Stephanie and I, as we thought about the history of this relationship and what we had seen, heard, and felt during our visit two years ago, concluded that diving in deeper was not our choice but rather a calling that was given to us. As members of Reba Place, we were born into this."

As Jesus was hanging on the cross he turned to the disciple he loved, nodded at his own mother Mary, and said, "Here is your mother."

"From that hour," the gospel of John tells us, "the disciple took her into his own home" (John 19:27).

In like fashion the Holy Spirit has said to the members of SMC communities and to the people of Valle Nuevo, "Here is your family." Whether we are naturally born or adopted into families, we do not choose our own family members. That is as true in the body of Christ as it is in tribes or clans or in nuclear or extended families.

There is no "been there done that" when it comes to family. None of us get tired of seeing our loved ones, and, if they live at a great distance, we will make great sacrifices to visit them. Repetition of family traditions and practices increase our sense of identity and help build unity. We take the bread and the cup again and again. "Do this in remembrance of me," Jesus commanded, and communion—laden with truth and memory and ever more meaningful each and every time we participate—is an endless walk of life and light. It is no surprise that Adam would return to El Salvador.

The people of God used symbols to help them remember events, pledges, and covenants long before Jesus picked up the bread and the cup. One year on the hike to the Lempa Joel Scott, with the age-old tradition of memory markers in mind, took a handful of stones from the river bank and asked Rosa Torres if he could take them back to Hope Fellowship. Rosa smiled, pleased at the request, and responded, "Just remember the blood that was shed."

SECTION 2: PRACTICES OF A TRANSNATIONAL COMMUNION

> ### Memories at the Lempa
>
> It was good to be accompanied on the journey down to the Lempa by several Salvadorans who had made the pilgrimage in 1981 as they fled for their lives. Several of the women sat on a big rock and looked very deep in thought. I was moved to see how somber and quiet Felipa was as she sat there. I went over to sit near her and listen a bit to her story. This was the first time she had returned to the Lempa after thirty years! Her husband Salomé had returned for the first time with the delegation last year. It was quite sobering to realize the depth of the pain that is still very real and challenging to face.
>
> RUTH ANNE FRIESEN, REBA PLACE FELLOWSHIP

Remembering the blood that was shed, whether it was at Golgotha or the Lempa, is not merely historical recall. It is a spiritual, social, and political act. It is spiritual because it transcends the obstacles of time and geography. Memory vanquishes "gone" and "left;" it overcomes separation and death. Remembering is also social, connecting not only the rememberer with the remembered but also increasing fraternity among the group of rememberers. When Christians take the Eucharist or when the Shalom Mission communities gather to commemorate Valle Nuevo's flight across the Lempa, they are building their corporate identity as the people of God.

And this type of remembering is political; it negates the power of sin that divides and separates. The early churches in the Roman empire understood that when they as Jew and Greek, slave and free, male and female sat down at the table together they were defying the social stratification of the Roman empire. Remembering is an assault on the hostility of a border; it takes the cup of the new covenant and creates community.

> ### In the Ditches There is Blood
>
> We are talking about this history, and in this story there is blood. The dead have struggled and given their lives without so much as a place to lay their heads. In the ditches there is blood, and we are cleaning out those ditches. Our effort for clarity in our communities is not just about putting beans and corn on the table, but as *Monseñor* Romero said, it is so we can have the Lord's Prayer at the table. In the ditches there is blood, and we are cleaning out those ditches.
>
> TOMASA TORRES, VALLE NUEVO

In her addresses and workshops during the 2015 SMC reunion, Juana Lainez, the first member of Valle Nuevo in eleven years to obtain a visa and attend the event, repeatedly reminded everyone of the other five who were denied visas. "We are family. In God's world there are no borders," she declared.

> ### Looking Forward to Friendship
>
> Remembering is essential to building relationship! What are the tangible ways we can remember our brothers and sisters in Valle Nuevo?
>
> - remember special dates (March 18, October 29) and special events/efforts in their community (planting, harvesting, weather with regards to agriculture, the anti-mining work, university students and their studies, the land legalization process)
> - have a quarterly pupusa night
> - e-mail/facebook (many of the youth and university students have internet access)
> - call (most have phones)
> - include a regular section in our "Shalom Connections" about our family in Valle Nuevo
> - keep up with the news about El Salvador and Central America
> - have framed pictures around our home of our "family" in Valle Nuevo
> - go on delegation trips
> - work on learning Spanish

Section 2: Practices of a Transnational Communion

> These are a few ways of "walking uphill" in search of friendship. May our Lord be honored as we remember our brothers and sisters in Valle Nuevo, as we build friendships and come to the banquet table together.
>
> *Nancy Gatlin, Hope Fellowship*

In the first dozen years of our relationship Yvonne Dilling was our bridge across the chasm. After Yvonne returned to live in the United States and SMC continued to visit, it became clear to everyone that the relationship would endure. As a result remembering has become less of a plea and more a practice, truly a fact of life. Still being remembered is not taken for granted. We all know that it takes work and that for the memories to become substantial and powerful the relationship itself must be passed on to future generations. When we are fully secure in the permanence of the "we," when sin, division, and borders are no more, we will plant a marker in memory of the former chasm whose nothingness has been exposed.

Chapter 7

Proclaiming

> For as often as you eat this bread and drink the cup,
> you proclaim the Lord's death until he comes.
>
> 1 Corinthians 11:26

Joanne and Rosa on the path to the Lempa

Section 2: Practices of a Transnational Communion

THE BRIGHT, MIDDAY SALVADORAN sun had beaten down all conversation by the time the pilgrims arrived at the riverside. People clustered in groups of two or three or four, some sitting uncomfortably on the sharp edges of boulders where shrubby trees provided scant shade and others leaning at awkward angles so that exposed body parts could share umbrellas. It was June 30, 2011, the Thursday trip to the Lempa during the annual SMC delegation visit.

Each year there is much that is the same when we go to the river. We always go in Carlos's vans and usually Carlos himself, who was one of the refugees and now lives just down the main street from Pastor and Rosa, drives one of them. The sun is invariably hot. For years we used the same trail down to the riverside, though some years it was a little muddy. The group is usually about half SMC delegates, both first-timers and many returnees, and half Valle Nuevo residents, both elders and young adults. The river itself is the same; it has not changed course. And once we are at the bank, the emotions that wash over us—immense in their impact on our fragile consciences and sharper than the edges of the boulders upon which we perch—are not new.

> ### An Afternoon with Margarita
>
> It is good to remember these stories [about the chapter draft from this book she had just received]. I made two colones a month. My job was to milk the cows. There was no man around except my uncle. I started working when I was twelve.
>
> I would get up a three in the morning to grind the corn on rock. Of course, I was younger then and had more energy. We lived on the bottom of the land. My mother had other daughters, but not all of them liked to work. My father died when I was eight.
>
> God called us to organize ourselves and ask for our rights. Through God's word we began to organize ourselves. Some men came and read from the Bible. This encouraged us to realize that at least the men should earn five colones a day. The rich people gave information to the military. They said, these people are disrupting our life. The military responded with bullets. That's how the war began.
>
> By that time, I had my young children.
>
> I had thought earlier they would just respond with understanding when we made our requests, but that was not the case. The military

> told the rich people, "We are going to silence them, to calm them." The movement actually began in 1933. The *campesinos* were all told to go to one place where their concerns would be addressed. They were shot down. The firefighters came and cleaned up the place and threw the bodies away with the garbage.
>
> I haven't been able to accomplish a whole lot in my life, but I've been able to see Christ. I taught first grade in Mesa Grande even though I only have a second-grade education. I've taught catechism. My favorite was teaching Bible to adults. I've also worked on a political party. I've worked a lot for the people. I did not just want to see the people dying.
>
> MARGARITA AVILEZ, VALLE NUEVO

As everyone caught their breath the silence grew. The glint of the sun's rays on the water's surface as it swept gently along the river's bend, the background of lush, green, growth ascending the hills on both banks, and the presence of good friends combined in concert to slow heartbeats and calm spirits. The reverence that welled up within the group, however, was more complex than an appreciation of the pastoral simplicity of the scene. SMC delegates as well as Valle Nuevo residents were being immersed, individually and collectively, into the profound depths of the river's contrasts. The Lempa's irenic beauty on a warm, summer day and its apocalyptic horrors flowing deep within its memories are two parts of one whole.

The experience is not unlike sitting in the elegantly simple chapel of Divina Providencia Hospital in the capital city. The sun's beatific rays softly illuminate the podium where Oscar Arnulfo Romero stood and held the chalice on the last day of his life. The non-conditioned-air is light and pleasant despite the heat and humidity outside, the presence of the Spirit is sublime, and it would be possible to sit in one of the pews for hours and just enjoy the peace. Near the door, however, are photographs taken just minutes after the Archbishop was shot. His body lies bleeding, some nuns hover over him, ministering to him, while others are springing up, calling for help. There is contrast between the beauty of the setting and the blood spilled on the floor and spattered on the nuns, between the serenity of the present moment and the chaos of that afternoon caught on black and white film almost forty years ago.

Section 2: Practices of a Transnational Communion

There is contrast but no discord. Winter, spring, summer, and fall define each other in their contrasts, but they also flow seamlessly through their transitions as parts of one integrated whole. So it is with the martyrdom of the Archbishop, the horror of March 18, the regeneration of June 30, and the formation of a transnational communion.

Within the Eucharist itself there is contrast. The words of institution in 1 Corinthians 11 close with Paul's theological interpretation given in verse 26 to the Christians in Corinth, "For as often as you eat this bread and drink the cup, you proclaim the Lord's death until he comes." Communion, that which joins and unifies, which re-members and serves as a declaration of the resurrection, is also a proclamation of death.

Serving each other bread and passing the cup around the table during the agape-love feast—as sweet as the experience was—did not complete the mission of the early Christian community in Corinth. In the Eucharist the struggle was re-embraced and the effort to cross the chasm was renewed. The darkness of the Roman empire yet surrounded them, brutality and violence were alive and well, their own deep-seated class divisions kept slipping back into their midst. The body of Christ must be constantly discerned and its wholeness rediscovered (1 Cor 11:28–29). Until Christ comes again, both then and now, those who confess his lordship will be proclaiming death on the cross.

Since the Catholic tradition of the *campesinos* requires a priest for the administration of the sacrament, we, this transnational communion, have never taken the Eucharist together. Our annual trip to the Lempa, however, is sacramental for in it we experience the administration of God's grace. This grace is not yet known in its fullness because we do not know the date the Lord will come again. For at least this season, and probably the next, our slender bridge across the chasm swings back and forth, hope and death and hope and death and hope and death. And hope. The last movement is always hope.

In the spring of 2013, Morena Ascencio, Salomé's and Felipa's daughter, was chosen as one of three Valle Nuevo residents who would apply to the United States Consulate for visas so they could travel to the Shalom Mission reunion to be held in Evanston that year. She later wrote this account of her experience.

> From the time I was a little girl I watched how we integrated the Shalom Mission delegations into the life of our community. I noticed how the adults in our community made preparations for these people who didn't seem like strangers but instead like true

friends. As time went on we made visits back and forth and the friendship grew. It felt as if the whole community was transporting itself there. I imagined how exciting it would be when it would be my turn to visit. I knew it would be one of their SMC gatherings so I would be able to get to know several of them at once.

My first application for a visa was denied because the authorities felt—since none of us had a job—we had insufficient funds to pay for our needs on this trip. Two years later when I attempted again I was confident I wouldn't have any problems. I had a job. I also had proof of study since I was in my fourth year of my early childhood licensing degree. And, of course, I had letters of invitation validating the purpose of the trip from the SMC coordinator and others. I worked hard to fill out my application completely. The three of us who were invited to travel decided to make the call to the Consulate as a group so we could get similar appointment times for our interview. It worked. We each were assigned the same day and time.

I rehearsed with my family what I would say and worked to prepare myself emotionally as well. The day before I rested a bit. It was the rainy season, and we knew there could be delays on the road so we had to leave early. The interview was set for nine which meant that I had to get up at three in the morning to be ready to leave for San Salvador at four.

As we arrived, we were at peace, yet eager to know what the Consul's response would be. I was sure this would be the day I would hear them say, "Yes, you may travel." All three of us, Juana, Pastor, and I, waited our turn. When it came, we each went to a different window since they required separate interviews. I greeted the man at the window cordially. He asked me the purpose of my trip. I explained I was invited to a church conference in which I had an official role. He then asked for proof of work and study, but had no other questions. I waited while he reviewed my documents. As I turned to where my partners had been, I realized they were no longer there. I wondered why my interview took longer. When my interviewer stood up after gathering my documents, he said, "Your visa is denied. We hope that at another time it will be possible." I thanked him for seeing me, and then with kindness I took my documents and left.

I felt a mix of emotions. My heart was beating hard, and I fought wanting to cry. But at the same time I told myself that I had to be strong for my partners because the three of us had done everything possible on our part. We were silent as we walked away. We couldn't believe it. We didn't speak until we got to the bus. We notified our families who were waiting to hear news, and then we let Nancy know. Even though they denied our visas, we believe it was worth the try. We never found out an answer as to why they denied us.

One day the chasm will be filled, every mountain and hill will be made low, the uneven ground will be leveled, and the rough places made into a plain (Isa 40:4). Or, to use another biblical image, one day the Lempa will become the river of the water of life, bright as crystal; death will be no more, and mourning and crying and pain will be no more (Rev 21:4; 22:1). For the meantime though, until the Lord comes again, we gather at the riverside and proclaim his death.

> ### The Bullet-Ridden Chair
>
> Life was really hard when we came here. The people in Santa Marta had settled around the soccer field. Because we came a little bit later we were on the outskirts and were able to breathe the air. But the conflict, the war, was still going on. We would build barricades to hide behind when the fire was going over our heads. We just crouched down when that was happening.
>
> I have a chair here that I've kept that has the bullet holes of where the bullets would come through our little house.
>
> I didn't think I was ever going to see my sons again. They weren't living here. They were living in other parts, and I thought we would be separated forever. But then the peace accords were signed, and shortly after that I was able to have my sons with me for a little while. I was so glad to see them. It was just amazing to be able to have them with me for a little while. One of my sons returned very affected by the civil war, and the only thing he could talk about was just the movements he made during the war. And it was just all about bullets and everything and that's all that he had in his head at that time. That's all he would talk about.
>
> And I remember there was this man from Spain who came and tried to get him out of that place in his head. He would take him out for walks, and he would try to get him away from this. And little by little he was able to a degree come out of that space that was just all about the war. And I had him here with me for a little while, but then he couldn't stay with me anymore.
>
> *Juana Lainez, Valle Nuevo*

Photographs rekindle memories of some of the unique experiences from each year's installment of the Lempa visit. We have a picture from 2011 of Joanne Janzen descending the rocky path with her arm draped over the shoulders of Rosa. Shortly before the trip Joanne had injured her foot back home in Evanston, but she was not going to be denied the pilgrimage to the Lempa. Rosa anticipated Joanne's difficulty and walked behind her until it was evident she needed support.

It was thirteen years since Joanne had traveled to Valle Nuevo and the Lempa. For Salomé, 2011 was his first return to the river in twenty years. A photo of him stoically gazing over the water captures the solemnity of the moment. Salomé was motionless and silent for some time before he was ready to share his reflections.

Thirty years earlier (plus three months and twelve days to be exact), at the very spot where in 2011 our communion of *campesinos* and communitarians rested, government death squads with the full support and funding of the United States government caught up with the fleeing refugees and dispensed chaos and death. Although the emotions vary greatly in intensity and depth, we all share sadness and loss as we witness this site of inexpressible evil.

Those who were there at ground zero on March 18, 1981, will forever carry the memory of horrified faces, bleeding wounds, screams, explosions, bullets whizzing by, and the thrashing arms of family members and friends being carried away by the waters. They mourn the loss of the warm touch of those loved ones who perished that day.

Those who were too young to remember or who were later born in the refugee camps or in the repatriated community of Valle Nuevo are a pivotal generation. As children, they naturally minister to their elders who yet bear unhealed wounds, both physical and emotional, while at the same time they are responsible for the survival, growth, and welfare of a community that was founded in death and deprivation. Perhaps the memories could just drift away down the river, past the bend, out of sight, carrying away their spiritual heaviness, but they know that March 18, just as with Good Friday more than two-thousand years ago, should forever be preserved in their collective consciousness as the defining moment of their peoplehood.

And for those from the north, there is the empathy that is felt for family, for dear friends, and for any human being who suffers. Tears evoke tears.

Shame is another powerful emotion that was present in the group gathered at the river. The *campesinos* have inherited a deep sense of inferiority that was formed during their generations of serfhood on the Salvadoran plantations and then greatly exacerbated during the civil war by the profoundly unsettling realization that other human beings saw them as nothing more than animals that could be slaughtered with impunity. This debilitating sense of disgrace has been passed on to the second and third generations.

Those from the United States carry a different sense of shame, one rooted in guilt; they are mortified and embarrassed about their government's active sponsorship of the war. Some of the older delegates during the seventies and eighties found ways to protest through demonstrations, tax resistance, or other means, but these were ineffective. They were left with a sad shaking of the head, a prayer of anguish, and ultimately a cry of the soul over that which they could not control. Their country's dehumanization of the *campesinos* is contemporary as well as historical, witness the ongoing denial of visas for Salvadoran visits to the United States.

In 2010 Nancy Gatlin set up an interview for the SMC delegation to discuss the visa issue with the United States Deputy Consul in San Salvador. That June, after background checks and clearance through the Embassy security protocols, six of the SMC delegates were ushered into the Consul's office. They began by asking why the visa applications for Valle Nuevo residents to come to the biannual SMC reunion were consistently rejected.

The officer politely explained that because of the enormous number of applications, the agents have only a few minutes to complete each in-person interview. As a result they consider only one factor, economic means, with three tests, evidence of a salary, a bank account, and title to real estate. Our applicants failed all three. As *campesinos* they are self-employed. As residents of Valle Nuevo of Santa Marta, they have no local bank. As resettled refugees, they had no titles to their homes and agricultural plots due to arcane, feudalistic laws and incomplete land reform. With these tests, not even a thousand letters of support would overcome the presumption that they are so poor they will be tempted to overstay a visa and make the United States home.

Someone from SMC wryly pointed out that the *campesinos* were in good company; Jesus himself would have failed these standards and been rejected. The officer, though, seemed genuinely interested in SMC's relationship with Valle Nuevo and said that for the next reunion, if he was still assigned to the Salvadoran consulate, he would flag their applications for personal attention. Three years later when SMC reunion preparations were again underway the officer had left, but prior to his departure he let Nancy know he had alerted others in the consulate about the SMC-Valle Nuevo connection. Nevertheless, the results were still the same; all of the applications, including Morena's, were cursorily denied.

SMC sent a letter of protest to the consulate and received the following reply from the Non-Immigrant Visa Chief Consular Section in the San Salvador embassy:

> Our Communications Unit responds to many e-mails over the course of a week, but I wanted to respond to you on a more personal level because you invested time in this effort, and you seem to have a good understanding of the challenges we face in adjudicating these difficult cases. You also ask a fair question: "What can we do to have our friends join us in our gatherings as we do yearly with them in El Salvador?"
>
> . . . After considering the totality of the applicants' circumstances, purpose of travel included, the applicants were not able to overcome the presumption of immigrant intent, which is one of the legal guidelines that our officers must follow.
>
> We know your organization has the best of intentions, and sharing your story or information on future applicants continues to be a good way for you to assist them. However please know that at the end of the day this is only part of the picture of every applicant, and each case is decided on its own merit based on the totality of the circumstances.

Representatives from the SMC communities discussed the letter in a conference call, and reminded themselves that as U.S. citizens the Consul is their employee. Nancy responded with a letter that opened with the appropriate pleasantries and then went on to say:

> . . . the last two of the Valle Nuevo residents who were denied . . . received a very quick "denied" with no opportunity to show evidence of their merits. As with previous attempts we in Shalom Mission Communities spent money for the visa process, but costlier was the time and loss of dignity for our Salvadoran friends who felt brushed aside despite their efforts to prepare themselves well for the interview.
>
> Our friends are economically poor, and that will probably not change much. They are, however, committed to their community. They gave up the opportunity to emigrate to other countries when they were in refugee camps in Honduras, but they chose to return to El Salvador. After a fifteen-year process to get their residential and agricultural lands legalized, they are now just months away from completing the process. We would hope and expect that the Consulate would hear their stories and their testimonies and read their letters of reference and be able to discern that their stability and

permanent status in their community. Their intent cannot be simply discerned by a two-minute evaluation of their financial condition.

Our question remains, what can we do to have our friends join us in our gatherings as we do yearly with them in El Salvador?

Morena's question—why were the visas rejected—was answered. The *campesinos* did not meet the economic means tests. However, the answer to the SMC question—what can we do to have our friends join us—was insufficient. "Sharing your story or information on future applicants continues to be a good way for you to assist them . . . " was producing only the smallest of results.

In June 2017, Dawn, Nancy, and Joe once again visited the U.S. Embassy in San Salvador and met with the Consul who politely confirmed the conclusion we had drawn that there actually is not much that United States citizens can do. The challenge is for the *campesinos* in their three-minute interview to overcome the presumption of "immigrant intent." Everyone, the Consul explained, must convince the interviewing officer they have compelling reasons to return home. Their reason for going is secondary.

"We will continue attempting to invite our friends who have become family to us," the communitarians have told the consular officers. Those of us on the north side of the border will continue to advocate for a more humane and inclusive U.S. immigration policy. We, all of us from both Valle Nuevo and SMC, will work to better prepare the *campesinos* for their interviews. We cannot change history, but we can all pray and work to change the conditions that separate us. As we proclaim the Lord's death, we pray for forgiveness, both that we may receive it and that we may extend it. The cancellation of debts, the remission of pain, the erasure of guilt, we all desire these.

"For as often as you eat this bread and drink this cup . . . " Paul told the early Christians. "Often" must mean with some degree of frequency and consistency. "For as often" rises above sporadic impulse; it does not mean just "Oh, whenever you get around to it."

Our annual trips to the Lempa are not as frequent as communion should be, but they are deliberate and purposeful. On that sweltering day in June, 2011, Nancy sat reflecting on the sacredness of the river and the solemnness of the spirit and with inspiration, yet some uncertainty, asked the group if they would be open to washing each other's feet. The *campesinos* had never experienced foot-washing before, but they were aware of the story of how Jesus showed his great love for his friends by getting down on his hands and knees as a slave and washing their dusty feet (John 17).

There was a moment of silence as everyone contemplated the possibility, and then Salomé, theologian and humorist, jumped up and making as though he was taking off his shirt, exclaimed as the Apostle Peter did on that evening more than two thousand years ago "Yes, not only my feet, but my whole body."

There on the bank of the Lempa, the victims and the executioners, those whose blood had been spilled into its waters thirty years earlier and those whose tax dollars paid for the bullets that tore into human bodies, washed each other's feet. One could imagine that Jesus had just returned. David Janzen, who was also part of the delegation that year, shared with those present that we do not wash our hands of responsibility in the face of injustice as Pilate did before the crucifixion of Christ. Instead we wash one another's feet "as a way to show that death, pain, and loss do not have the last word, but rather the last word is reconciliation through mutual servanthood as followers of Jesus."

> ### A Reflection on Washing Feet at the Lempa
>
> The SMC delegates were eager to serve as hands of healing to those who had suffered trauma and loss at the river, but felt more awkward in allowing their feet to be washed by the *campesinos*. My hope is that their example will cause us to pause and recognize our need to repent of the ways in which we have charged on ahead, sitting down and gorging ourselves at a table of plenty while others remain hungry. We need to take a long, hard look at our own economic prosperity. In what ways do we contribute to the hunger of others because we have piled up our own plates too high?
>
> If we truly want to live in solidarity with our friends and offer them a place at the banquet table of basic health care, education, nutrition, and adequate housing, then we need to find a place to meet. We will have to backtrack on this trail that has led us to such abundance to find our brothers and sisters and walk together, holding each other up when necessary, on a new path to a place where there is enough for everyone and 'no one will lack what is needed.' We must leave our obscenely abundant wealth behind and seek to change this way of life that necessitates war and oppression in order to sustain it.
>
> DAWN NOELLE SMITH BEUTLER,
> CHURCH OF THE SOJOURNERS

SECTION 2: PRACTICES OF A TRANSNATIONAL COMMUNION

The Apostle Paul, just a few paragraphs after the words of institution, rhapsodized about the power of love, "Love does not rejoice in wrongdoing, but rejoices in truth. It bears all things, believes all things, hopes all things, endures all things" (1 Cor 13:6–7). Valle Nuevo and SMC on the bank of the Lempa bore witness to that truth. There was a vision of the chasm filled.

> **Vamos Todos al Banquete**
>
> Strong *campesinos*
> with dark eyes and lean frames
> teach gringo friends
> how poor and weak we are.
> Planting rows of corn
> on steep green hillsides
> they've waited so long to own,
> they lay claim to the land
> God has given them to steward.
> Feeding young minds with education,
> they sow a crop to grow
> a new generation of leaders
> who will not forget their martyrs
> nor their deliverance
> yet are moving forward
> to claim the banquet is for all.
> In the meantime
> we wash each others' feet
> with tears and living water,
> receiving what we need
> as companions
> on our journey together.
>
> SALLY SCHREINER YOUNGQUIST, REBA PLACE.
> SALLY HAS NOT BEEN ABLE TO GO ON A DELEGATION.

That fall of 2011, in one of the Waco coffee shop meetings on this book project, Nancy shared again with Joe and Joel, who had not gone on the delegation that year, the experience of the foot-washing and the perennial *despedida* refrain always shared by Pastor and others: "We thank you so much for coming. Please don't forget us."

Nancy looked down at the table and shook her head, "They don't understand. We don't go for them; we go for us."

"Perhaps," Joe said, "we could use the parable of Lazarus and the rich man. That would make it very clear why we go."

Within the next few months the metaphor of "Crossing the Great Chasm" emerged as a theme for this book. Discussions stateside led to the conclusion that the *directiva* would need to give its input and approval. There was concern that the brothers and sisters of Valle Nuevo would feel diminished by the obvious analogy of their situation to that of Lazarus, the poor man covered with sores, stuck outside the gate.

In the last ten years our time for theological reflection has come to be one of the highlights of the delegation visits. It is simple enough. One of the SMC members will read a passage of Scripture and then with a short introduction about the Biblical context and the struggle to understand and apply this back home, asks, "What do you think?" Some of the individual Valle Nuevo leaders at times will claim they are not religious people, but all of them are remarkably familiar with Scripture and very insightful in knowing how to apply it.

In 2012, on the night of the *despedida*, Joe—with some trepidation—shared, "You have often asked us why we come to visit you. There are many reasons; we receive so much from you and this relationship. Let me use a Bible story to tell you one reason." He then proceeded to read the story of the Great Chasm from Luke 16.

"What do you think of this story?" he asked the members of the *directiva*.

There was hardly a moment of silence, and then the circle exploded with enthusiasm, chattering excitement, and shining eyes. "Oh, we know that parable," said Pedro almost coming up out of his chair. "We know it well; we like this parable" and heads around the circle nodded yes. "We have a song about it!" he looked and saw that all of the members of the *directiva* were with him. There was laughter, and then they all broke into an obviously happy song about Lazarus and the rich man.

"This parable is good news!" exclaimed Juana.

"We know who we are in this parable," added Pastor. "We are Lazarus, the poor man." And everyone nodded their heads up and down. These affirmations continued for a while with everyone laughing and enjoying the moment.

Joe broke into the conversation and said, "Yes, we know who we are too in this parable. We are the rich man, and we are on the wrong side of the chasm for the hereafter. That's why we come here now. You think we come here to help you, but that is not true. We are the ones who need you."

For another hour conversation continued about the nature of the chasm and the relevant experiences of those from the south and those from the north and what it meant to cross the chasm. At one point as the evening was wrapping up, Pastor turned to Joe who was sitting beside him and said with the utmost sincerity and empathy, with no hint of sarcasm, "I know it must be difficult to be rich."

Paul concluded his instructions on communion with these words, "Whoever, therefore, eats the bread or drinks the cup of the Lord in an unworthy manner will be answerable for the body and blood of the Lord. Examine yourselves, and only then eat of the bread and drink of the cup. For all who eat and drink without discerning the body, eat and drink judgment against themselves. . . . So then, my brothers and sisters, when you come together to eat, wait for one another" (1 Cor 11:27–29; 33).

> ### One Can't Carry the Cross Sitting Down
>
> One can't carry the cross sitting down; we march with the Gospel towards the light of God! We are secure in the reality of God. Through you we have a million friends!
>
> *Tomasa Torres, Valle Nuevo*

The people of Shalom Mission Communities have apologized, and they will apologize again. The feeling of unworthiness carried by the people of Valle Nuevo is not easy to shake off. Our business is unfinished.

We confess sin and we proclaim Christ's death. "For now we see in a mirror dimly," Paul also wrote to the church in Corinth. On one side of the chasm there is destitution today. And tomorrow there may be destitution on the other side. But one day "we will see face to face" (1 Cor 13:12).

Section 3

The Table of Creation

Vamos Todos al Banquete/Let's Go Now to the Banquet

Vamos todos al banquete,	Let's go now to the banquet,
A la mesa de la creación,	To the table of creation,
Cada cual con su taburete	Where each one with their own chair
Tiene un puesto y una misión.	Has a place and a mission to share.
Hoy me levanto muy temprano,	I will rise in the early morning,
Ya me espera la comunidad;	The community's waiting for me;
Voy subiendo alegre la cuesta,	With joy I'm walking up the hill,
Voy en busca de tu amistad.	Looking forward to your friendship.
Dios invita a todos los pobres	God invites all the poor
A esta mesa común por la fe,	To the common table of faith,
Donde no hay acaparadores	Where there are none hoarding the harvest
Y a nadie le falta el conqué.	and no one will be in need.
Dios nos manda hacer de este mundo	God charges us to make of this world
Una mesa donde haya igualdad;	A place where all are equal in love.
Trabajando y luchando juntos,	We work and struggle together,
Compartiendo la propiedad.	And share everything we have.

Chapter 8

Lessons Learned
Celebration, Companionship, Community, and Courage

For he is our peace; in his flesh he has made both groups into one and has broken down the dividing wall, that is, the hostility between us.

Ephesians 2:14

A meal on Pastor and Rosa's verandah

Section 3: The Table of Creation

We entered 2016 with high hopes the SMC annual delegation visit would be capped by a fiesta celebrating the legal titling of the homes and agricultural properties of 171 Valle Nuevo families. For a people who were treated as chattel for generations, who fled from their homes to escape their government's effort to exterminate them, and who struggled to survive for almost a decade in refugee camps, the prospect of owning their own land was an enormous, gigantic, profoundly significant, and revolutionary hope. No stream of superlatives can capture completely the importance of secure tenure for those who have always been—at least within the reaches of their collective memory and recorded history—without the gate.

The delegation visit did close with a fiesta that year despite the fact that there were no land titles. Our lessons learned have to do with faithfulness, regardless the circumstances and what may appear to be setbacks. God is faithful. Therefore, we should always celebrate, we should always accompany each other, we should always recognize that our wealth is communal property, and we should always be courageous. Stories from the last two days of the twenty-fifth SMC annual delegation to Valle Nuevo capture the importance of these lessons: celebration, companionship, community, and courage. The larger context is the journey toward land legalization in Valle Nuevo.

The land campaign had begun in 1992 just a few months after the first SMC visit to Valle Nuevo. The *directiva* asked for help to acquire agricultural fields on the side of El Picacho, a mountain just to the north of the community, so they could grow enough corn and beans for their own survival. Reba Place and Plow Creek responded by eventually raising $34,000, and the site was purchased and held communally by Valle Nuevo. Clear title, however, was not achieved; post-war attempts at national land reform had been—and would continue to be—inadequate in overcoming a feudalistic history and legal system that supported the property rights of fourteen wealthy families who had controlled all land in El Salvador. No one was moving the *campesinos* and the crops off the side of the mountain, but until the legalities could be accomplished, their stake would always seem tenuous. Moreover, the ownership of the residential properties had not been addressed at all. Valle Nuevo's existence on the face of the earth seemed like a wisp of smoke, ready to vanish with the gentlest of breezes.

In 2004 the *directiva*, Shalom Mission, and others initiated an effort with a new lawyer to legally title the lots, but before long the process slowed and at times moved backwards rather than forward. Over the next several years legalization efforts proceeded in fits and starts as new bumps and twists regularly appeared. One of the bright spots was Habitat's willingness in 2006 to launch the housing effort in Valle Nuevo and Santa Marta even though titles were still not clear.

In 2008 the *directiva* requested help in fundraising another $26,000 in order to hire an engineer who would survey and parcel the eleven large tracts into both residential and agricultural individual family plots. SMC was able to meet the request, and, with the addition of the residential lots to the package, Habitat El Salvador stepped in as the fiduciary for the project.

> ### How to Manage $25,000
>
> They asked, "Brothers and sisters in solidarity, can you help us raise the money?" We prayed together and said "yes."
>
> "This, we believe, is what God wants." Our communities were poor, but we raised what we could and asked many friends, including children, to pitch in. A few months later we sent $25,000 as a down payment, enough to close the deal.
>
> The men of Valle Nuevo wondered, "How can we get all this cash to the lawyer's office without being robbed by soldiers or bandits?" The problem was solved by typical *campesino* genius—a couple of women carried all this cash across the town of Sensuntepeque to the lawyer's office in ordinary market baskets with towels over the top as if they were full of tortillas.
>
> DAVID JANZEN, REBA PLACE FELLOWSHIP

A new land reform law in 2012 promised to shorten the process, seemingly great news, until someone did the math on a tax of one cent per square-meter. An additional $19,000 would have to be raised to pay this bill. The *directiva*, SMC, Habitat, and the lawyer discussed and decided to seek an alternate route rather than trying to raise more funds. With support from the governor of Cabañas they were able to recruit assistance from the Instituto de Legalización de la Propiedad (the Institute of Property Legalization or ILP), a government agency working to help low-income communities achieve secure tenure in their land.

Although the ILP had never taken on a project of this magnitude with so many parties and parcels of land, it agreed to the challenge. By the close of 2015, with the ILP's professional specialists working under the auspices of the government, it seemed that all major obstacles had been removed. Throughout the first part of 2016, Nancy was regularly on the phone with

Section 3: The Table of Creation

various members of the *directiva* and Habitat as everyone tried to push the land titling toward consummation. In the spring additional obstacles and issues began to emerge, but all held onto hope for the June closing.

Valle Nuevo and SMC began to plan for the mother of all parties to celebrate formal signing during the June delegation. A number of SMC members—some who had not been to Valle Nuevo for several years and others who never been able to go—held up their hands. David Janzen thought it might be his last trip to Valle Nuevo. Jim Fitz wanted to return as well as other more recent delegation regulars like Adam Vaughan and Carol Youngquist. Barb Grimsley from Reba, who had thought for a number of years that the trip might be too arduous, was enticed to sign up. Clare Bridgewater, Julia Coyne, and Jaden Janzen, teenagers from Hope Fellowship and Reba, were interested. E-mails between the Shalom communities flew back and forth in the final two months.

Finally, at six weeks out, even though some challenges remained, plane tickets were purchased for fourteen delegates, a larger group than usual. Party supplies that could be packed into suitcases were bought, and other trip preparations were made.

As it came to pass, however, about three weeks prior to the delegation there still remained abnormalities with three of the families' titles that would prevent closing on three out of the eleven large tracts. In one case key individuals whose names were on earlier documents were now residing out of the country, and in the other two there was ambiguity about the legal status of marriages. Despite pressure from the ILP to go ahead and close those that were ready, the *directiva* with a typical show of *campesino* solidarity decided there would be no closings until all were closed. Their concern was that in the rush to closure and celebration of the majority, energy would be lost for completing the details on the remaining parcels.

By June 1, we had to acknowledge we would not get the ball across the goal line. No one was that surprised; there were so many times in the last decade we had thought we were close, only again to be disappointed.

Nancy and Dawn and the *directiva* worked to make adjustments in the delegation schedule, and everyone agreed a party should still close out the week. David Janzen volunteered to put together a slide show celebrating our twenty-five years. The ceremony for signing the titling documents was scratched, and in its place a Wednesday meeting in Valle Nuevo was scheduled with representatives of the ILP and Habitat with hopes that all

Lessons Learned

of the parties together in one room could find solutions to the outstanding issues and provide energy for the final push.

When the SMC delegates arrived in Valle Nuevo they communicated their sympathy to the *directiva* that once again efforts had been thwarted. Pastor and others responded, "Oh we are fine. We are used to this. We've been very afraid you would be sad because we know you too have worked so hard on the land titling."

In the meeting on Wednesday the *directiva* was able to express clearly the community's need to stay in solidarity by waiting until all of the parcels could be closed. Several other *non-directiva* families also showed up for the meeting to voice their support. The other parties present—the ILP and Habitat representatives and the SMC delegates—were able to appreciate the importance of maintaining unity among the *campesinos*.

The meeting quickly moved into a problem-solving mode with concrete steps identified and responsibilities assigned. At the close everyone affirmed their commitment to complete the final steps by mid-August. Valle Nuevo and SMC wished their ILP and Habitat colleagues safe travels back to San Salvador on that Wednesday afternoon and then turned to the events of the remaining two days of the delegation and its culmination with the Friday afternoon fiesta.

From a human point of view a celebration was not in order. Not only did the people of Valle Nuevo lack secure tenure, their water supply, both in quantity and quality, was in critical condition. A stable economy was as elusive as ever. The youth were in crisis due to safety and violence issues and departures to the United States. Who, we all wondered, as we surveyed the group of younger people in the room, would still be in the community the following June and who would be languishing in an immigration detention center in south Texas? Who might be dead due to gang violence? And fragility was not just an issue for Valle Nuevo; the future of a couple of the Shalom communities with aging populations and leadership transitions looked unsure.

"When there is communion between people they sometimes work together," Jean Vanier the founder of the L'Arche communities wrote, "but what matters to them is not that they succeed in achieving some target, but simply that they are together, that they find their joy in one another and care for one another." It was Wednesday afternoon. We still had two days of the delegation visit left, and we were going to party. *Vamos todos al banquete*—come let's go to the banquet. We would party, regardless of what had been accomplished or not.

Section 3: The Table of Creation

LESSON 1: CELEBRATION

Vamos todos al banquete,	Let's go now to the banquet,
A la mesa de la creación,	To the table of creation,
Cada cual con su taburete	Where each one with their own chair
Tiene un puesto y una misión.	Has a place and a mission to share.

Bring the fattened calf and kill it. Let's have a feast and celebrate.

Luke 15:23

On Thursday morning at 7:30 the two microbuses started picking up people at Pastor's and Rosa's house at the bottom of the hill. By the time we had climbed out of the valley we were twenty-eight, fourteen from SMC and fourteen from Valle Nuevo, packed in tightly enough that we were cushioned from the hard jolts of the rough, rocky road that would carry us to the Lempa.

Half of the Valle Nuevo representatives were from the youth group, a practice we had instituted several years earlier. For several of them it was their first trip ever to the storied riverside that two generations earlier defined their history and still colored their present.

At the river a new project was underway. A father, his young son, and another boy from the community were hauling rocks up the hill from the riverbank in order to build a long staircase to the actual spot where the *campesinos* scrambled down to the river of death in 1981. The father's vision was to memorialize the Lempa by making it possible for the elders to still descend the hill and stand by its side.

As usual, it was a hot day and the humidity hung on us. When we were about three-quarters of the way down we found a shady spot that provided a panoramic view of the river. As we've done so many times, we sat silently and contemplated life, pain, suffering, death, loss, guilt, endings, and beginnings. Several began to share some of their thoughts.

Juana recalled more specifics, how in the confusion of that horrible day she had to climb back up the hill looking desperately for family members. As others of the older generation told their stories again, everyone could feel the chaos, the stumbling descent, the noise of the gunfire and human screams, and what seemed like the end of the world.

The youth were silent; their faces were impassive. It was difficult to tell what they were thinking or feeling. Were they bored with the stories, some of us wondered. Were they just ready to move on?

LESSONS LEARNED

> ### Calm and Anguish
>
> This place is very calm today. I can feel it. But I know the grief that was here. This place is also full of nostalgia. This is my second time here. I know only what my mother has told me about this place. I imagine the screaming and anguish and wonder if I would have survived.
>
> KATY MEJÍA, A VALLE NUEVO YOUTH

Heydi Ayala López broke their silence. "We are eternally linked," she began as tears welled in her eyes. "I am here because of a miracle. My father was the only survivor in a group that was killed. My grandmother crossed by herself with four children, one of whom was my mother. She was nine." The specifics of her story belong to a child of war refugees, but in her reverence and recognition of the miracle of the divine, of redeeming the tragedy of the past by recognizing its gift of the present, of claiming community with those who have gone before us, she represented all of us.

The other young people began to talk as well as more of the adults. The horror was not forgotten, but as more shared, SMC delegates as well as *campesinos*, the emotion shifted from the grief of loss to marvel and celebration of the wonder of life.

> ### Before and After the War
>
> Before the war we worked the land and we were only able to keep half of what we grew. The other half went to the landlord. We were sick. We worked long hours. We were hungry. We died young. We had no school. We received no education.
>
> Today we have a good clinic. We have a good school. We can organize ourselves and have meetings. We can make decisions. Our children can go to the university. I can raise chickens and sell eggs. We have you for our friends.
>
> JUANA LAINEZ, VALLE NUEVO

Even though pain and suffering are always present, we realized, we are here together—young and old, *campesino* and communitarian, south and north—on the same side of the gate. Our transnational communion

SECTION 3: THE TABLE OF CREATION

has come about because of a series of events, saints, and circumstances that defy comprehension unless we attribute them to the divine.

We were ready to celebrate because:

- an obscure, passive, quiet priest was appointed Archbishop and then heard God's call,
- Margarita perceived the pillar of light as the *campesinos* made their escape,
- Angelina survived submersion in the Lempa for three days,
- Yvonne, a champion swimmer and a person of empathy and compassion, was present at the river on March 18, 1981,
- David crossed paths with Yvonne at the exact moment he was seeking divine direction,
- Nancy and Dawn with their unique gifts stepped forward to provide leadership for the relationship at the moment it was needed,
- Carlos and Habitat for Humanity and Neil and World Hunger Relief were listening to God,
- Salomé, Pastor, Juana, Tomasa, Pedro, and others stood up and served as spokespeople for the community,
- Morena, Ana, Heydi, Fernando, and a host of other young people are taking on responsibilities in an important time of transition.

God had given us that day our daily bread. Even though the titles to the land had been delayed again, we were coming to the table of creation. The feast was ready and a place was waiting.

LESSON 2: COMPANIONSHIP

Hoy me levanto muy temprano,	I will rise in the early morning,
Ya me espera la comunidad;	The community's waiting for me;
Voy subiendo alegre la cuesta,	With joy I'm walking up the hill,
Voy en busca de tu amistad.	Looking forward to your friendship.

He called the twelve and began to send them out two by two. . . .

Mark 6:7a

Lessons Learned

Upon the return from the river the van dropped Nancy and Joe at Margarita's house at the top of the hill in *Las Brisas* neighborhood. Margarita, aware that Nancy's mother and father and Joe's mother had all passed away the previous year within a period of three months, had undertaken a novena, a nine-day series of prayers on behalf of the deceased. She had invited Nancy and Joe to join her and her neighbors for the closing service that Thursday, the one-year anniversary of the death of Nancy's mother.

As they entered the gate Margarita greeted them, walking slowly and with obvious discomfort. Her almost eighty-three-year-old eyes looked weaker than usual, and sweat was beaded across her forehead. Yes, she confirmed as they sat down to visit, she was not feeling well. It probably was chikungunya fever, a mosquito-borne virus that had visited almost everyone in the community.

At the appointed time of 4:30 they moved inside to her living room where her altar with candles, drapery, a Bible, and chaplets reached to the ceiling and took almost half of the floor-space. From an ornate picture frame placed at the top of the bamboo structure the Archbishop Romero's visage eternally watches over her home and her life. For the nine days of the novena a picture of the Virgin of Carmen, who pleads for those in purgatory, also graced the altar.

After the three of them were seated, Margarita rose stiffly, walked to the altar and came back with a white scrap of paper. "Look," she said, sitting once again and handing the paper to Nancy. "How do you say their names?"

The names of Joe's and Nancy's parents, 'Allene', 'James', and 'Peggy', were written in a shaky script. Nancy helped Margarita practice the names. Margarita then rose and went back to the altar, placing the paper once again at its center. She explained that Nancy and Joe should begin the novena with a prayer in their own tradition.

A few minutes later Miriam, Margarita's daughter, and another *campesina* arrived and took their places kneeling on the hard, concrete floor. Margarita, taking her rosary in her hands, nodded at Joe and Nancy who then offered up their prayers.

Everyone shut their eyes tightly. Margarita began, *"Dios te salve, María, llena eres de gracia, el Señor es contigo. Bendita tú eres entre todas las mujeres, y bendito es el fruto de tu vientre, Jesús. Santa María, Madre de Dios, ruega por nosotros pecadores, ahora y en la hora de nuestra muerte. Amén."*

The others responded, *"Gloria al Padre, al Hijo y al Espíritu Santo. Como era en el principio, ahora y siempre, por los siglos de los siglos. Amén."*

Section 3: The Table of Creation

The pattern continued, call and response, as Margarita fingered each of the rosary beads in turn. Other voices joined in. After about ten minutes Margarita paused, painfully straightening her back, and took the three or four short steps to the altar, retrieved the piece of paper, and brought it back to Nancy. Pointing her finger at the first name of the paper, she looked at Nancy seeking help.

"Allene," Nancy said.

"Allene," Margarita repeated, struggling with the English names, and nodded. And then she pointed at the next.

"James."

"James." And then the next.

"Peggy."

"Peggy."

Margarita turned and walked the list back to the altar. All eyes squinched shut again, and the prayers resumed with even greater fervor. For a total of forty-five minutes the pattern continued. More neighbors arrived until every available spot on the living room floor was occupied and others spilled out the door. Every ten minutes there was a pause for Margarita to get the paper and have Nancy help her pronounce the names of those who had died. The volume of the prayers increased until, suddenly, it was over. There was a moment of silence. The rosary was complete, the novena was fulfilled, and we all imagined Allene, James, and Peggy in the presence of God. Intercession had been made.

> ### Sacred Human Beings
>
> When we traveled to visit SMC communities and were called brothers and sisters, this reminded me of Jesus's words when he said about his family that those who do the will of my Father are my brothers and sisters. This is what it means to discern the body.
>
> *Tomasa Torres, Valle Nuevo*

With gratitude Nancy and Joe looked around the room and realized that a large group of *campesinos*, who knew them only by proxy through Margarita and had never met their parents, had just accompanied them up the hill to where the rest of the heavenly community was anticipating their arrival with great joy. At that same point a delicious plate of hot, fried yucca with *curtido*, a type of cole slaw that accompanies *pupusas* as well as most other *campesino* dishes, seemed to miraculously appear. Everyone in the room enjoyed the companionship around the eternal banquet table.

This relationship is about companionship. We do nothing alone. We follow Jesus together. We are in community in the south and in community in the north, and we create community in and over the chasm. We do not go on delegations alone. We do not travel alone. We are not refugees alone. We do not bear guilt alone. We do not cross the threshold of death alone. We call ourselves *compañeros*. In the here and the hereafter we are walking with families and friends.

LESSON 3: COMMUNITY

Dios invita a todos los pobres	God invites all the poor
A esta mesa común por la fe,	To the common table of faith,
Donde no hay acaparadores	Where there are none hoarding the harvest
Y a nadie le falta el conqué.	and no one will be in need.

> Now the whole group of those who believed were of one heart and soul, and no one claimed private ownership of any possessions, but everything they owned was held in common.
>
> Acts 4:32

That Thursday evening after the trip to the Lempa and after Nancy and Joe had attended the novena, the delegation dined with Felipa and Salomé and their family. Marga, Morena, and their sisters cooked a feast of *pastelistos*, tostadas, a fresh vegetable mix, and fried potatoes. Morena managed to find a corner seat at the long table otherwise completely filled by the fourteen delegates. Other members of the large, extended Ascencio family sat and ate in little groups in various corners of the verandah.

The delegates debriefed their day and shared emerging plans for Friday morning. Adam reported on the conversation he had just had with Salomé and Felipa's son-in-law Adonay; the two of them were planning a Friday morning hike to the Picacho so Adonay could show Adam more of his work. Matt Hess, the new Executive Director of World Hunger Relief who had joined the 2016 delegation, invited any who were ready for an early morning outing to visit the greenhouses. Matt also shared about a proposed World Hunger Relief delegation in November for board members and farm volunteers.

Section 3: The Table of Creation

After dinner the daily tropical storm began pounding on the roof of the verandah. The table was cleared, the younger delegates and the family youth sat back down for a game of UNO. The raucous laughter and squeals erupting from the gang indicated that language was no barrier.

Salomé, Felipa, Nancy, Dawn, Joe, Carol, Morena, Marga, and Matt retired into a distant corner where they could hear each other over the din of the card game and rain on the metal roof. It was not long before conversation drifted to a rehash of the previous day's meeting about land titles. Salomé explained more in depth how land passes from one generation to the next and the challenges that inevitably arise in particular circumstances of some families, for instance how to title land that belongs to a family unit composed of an elderly mother with two sons with debilitating mental illness resulting from the war.

At one point, the two, old, grizzled SMC veterans, David and Jim, who had first visited Valle Nuevo almost twenty-five years earlier, appeared and joined the corner group. "Were you napping?" Joe teased.

"No, just discussing the truth," Jim said with a wry smile, yet utter seriousness.

Truth. Joe and Nancy shared how deeply they had been moved by the novena earlier that afternoon. Salomé, Felipa, Marga, and Morena all nodded with understanding—understanding of the truth of Nancy's and Joe's emotion, of the compassion and solidarity expressed by Margarita and her neighbors, and of the providence of God.

Joe recalled how a few years earlier in November, he, Nancy, and Salomé sat at that very same spot on the Ascencio verandah when Salomé had prefaced his gratitude for a mountain of tortillas with the story of losing his brother during the war. And again, there had been the truth of compassion as Joe learned the news of his own brother's death while on that short trip to Valle Nuevo. Truth is being able to share suffering and death.

Nancy asked about Carlos and Jesús, the two Ascencio sons who were living in the United States. They were doing well, Felipa reported, but she missed them. Salomé, Marga, and Morena nodded. The truth was, Nancy and Joe knew from a stateside visit a couple of years earlier with their sons, Carlos and Jesús profoundly felt—perhaps even more than their parents in Valle Nuevo—the width and depth of the chasm of separation that prevented them from sitting on the verandah with their family members.

Lessons Learned

Nancy reminisced, "Salomé, do you remember what you said when you called to tell me that Carlos was somewhere in a detention center in south Texas?" Salomé looked uncertain.

"You told me I should consider him to be my own son," Nancy continued.

All in the circle sat in silence, contemplating the truth, the implications, and the blessing of this statement. Even our children belong to each other. We are one, not because the people of Valle Nuevo and Shalom Mission Communities are extraordinary or have discovered some mysterious secret about building a transnational relationship. We are one because we are made of the same flesh and the same bones. We are one because we have been purchased with the blood of Jesus Christ. We are one because we are born of the same Spirit. In that unity, one's need is everyone's need so the harvest is freely shared.

In the fullness of God's realm, when we are all sitting at the common table of faith, we will enjoy great diversity. There will be, however, one set of differences no longer in our circle, there will be no rich and no poor. Our communion will be profound. We will share all that we have, from harvest to farms to family and friends. We will not share money, however, because for that there will be no need.

On this side of the grave we do not know how to live perfectly in this gospel truth. Our communities in SMC attempt to actualize our oneness in Christ by building structures and systems and establishing patterns of economic sharing, yet we still deal in dollars and describe our exchanges and interchanges with terms and values defined by the principalities and powers of this world. Sometimes it looks like we are headed in the opposite direction. The economic disparity between the people of the south and the people of the north—when examined in the light of day—is still glaring and shocking.

Even though most days we may take one step back for every step forward, the truth is we are keeping our eyes on the vision. The Lord has brought us to the common table of faith where there is no hoarding.

Section 3: The Table of Creation

LESSON 4: COURAGE IS REQUIRED BY ALL

Dios nos manda hacer de este mundo	God charges us to make of this world
Una mesa donde haya igualdad;	A place where all are equal in love.
Trabajando y luchando juntos,	We work and struggle together,
Compartiendo la propiedad.	And share everything we have.

> For our struggle is not against enemies of blood and flesh, but against the rulers, against the authorities, against the cosmic powers of this present darkness, against the spiritual forces of evil in the heavenly places.
>
> Ephesians 6:12

On Friday afternoon, after some had hiked to the Picacho, some had visited the greenhouses and gardens, and some had just hung out and visited on the verandahs of various homes, everyone came back together at the communal house. It was time to party. Several gathered under a tree and played on the drum that Adam had brought the previous year and left with the community. Some started a rotating game of catch in the side yard with the ball and gloves he had brought along this year. Ana, Katy, Heydi, Kenya and others of the Valle Nuevo youth were showing to some of the SMC women the jewelry they had just finished making the afternoon before. Matt and Pastor and others scurried here and there to round up more chairs. Carol and Joe worked on the computer, projector, and electrical connections so we could all watch David's slide show. Dawn and Nancy compared notes for the agenda and consulted with Morena. All were pleased when Tomasa arrived knowing that it was not easy for her to break loose from caring for Felix, her husband. Salomé and Jim were deep in conversation in one corner. Rosa and others were arriving with large baskets of tamales they had made for the main meal.

Why We Do This

We do this because of Christ's command.

Salomé as he washed Joe's feet in the Lempa

It was a typical Salvadoran June afternoon with gathering tropical clouds. The first big raindrops signaled it was time for all to come inside.

Lessons Learned

Within seconds the rain was pounding hard on the metal roof. Dawn rose to welcome everyone, but since our available technology did not include a microphone and sound system, it was clear she could not compete with the reverberating drumfire of the downpour.

As though to stake our claim on a place in God's world, with no prompting our voices rose in unison above the din of the storm, and we sang all four verses of "*Vamos Todos*".

"*Dios nos manda hacer de este mundo una mesa donde haya igualdad*—God charges us to make of this world a place where all are equal in love. *Trabajando y luchando juntos, compartiendo la propiedad*—We work and struggle together, and share everything we have." The rain slowed and our program proceeded.

The work of creation is accomplished with words, for it is with words that we build relationships and shape the reality of the world by claiming God's presence, discerning the movement of the Spirit, pronouncing healing and forgiveness, articulating memories, declaring good, identifying evil, and confessing Jesus as Lord.

> ### The Everyday Challenges
>
> It seemed very natural. After all, she grew up in Salomé and Felipa's home. She talked about the challenge of raising teenage sons.
>
> DAWN NOELLE, REFLECTING ON HER FOOT-WASHING
> EXCHANGE WITH MARGARITA ASCENCIO

It takes courage to stand and speak in front of a group: individuals have to overcome shyness and stage fright, they have to believe their meanings and intents will transcend language differences, and they have to hope that what they are saying will not seem stupid or naive to others. Before the evening was over, youth, elders, middle-aged, new SMC delegates, veteran delegates, women, and men stood to share their blessings. There were stories of perseverance observed, compassion received, and new friendships commenced.

It takes courage in this material and secular world to name God as an actor. Our reflections were suffused with the theological. In his twenty-five-year photo history, a highlight of the evening, David spoke for all of us,

> In our old age we have returned to the Lempa River to once more remember God's deliverance, a story that must be passed on to the next generation both in El Salvador and in the United States. We

wash each others' feet as Jesus taught us, to wash away old griefs in this place and to make new memories of resurrected hope in mutual service. God is still with us in saints old and new, making us one family.

We have passed from death to life. We have crossed the chasm. We are not forgotten, and we are forgiven.

Chapter 9

Looking Forward: Our Call to Action

Not that I have already obtained this or have already reached the goal; but I press on to make it my own, because Christ Jesus has made me his own.

PHILIPPIANS 3:12

Fausto Torres and 170 more receive title to their land

IN TELLING THE STORIES of their great suffering, the people of Valle Nuevo are apt to quote George Santayana, "Those who cannot remember the past will be condemned to repeat it." Our transnational communion through

SECTION 3: THE TABLE OF CREATION

the passage of time offers a variation on this venerable saying, "Those who can see God's hand in their past will welcome the future with hope and joy."

On December 1, 2016, Shalom Missions received an email from Beatriz Bejarano, the Director of Operations for Habitat El Salvador.

> Finally, today, I received confirmation that the official presentation of the land titles for Valle Nuevo will take place on December 20, 2016. The Minister of Public Works, Housing, Transportation and Urban Development, Mr. Gerson Martínez, will deliver 412 titles, including both residential and agricultural lots.

North of the border email and Facebook posts spread the breathtaking news around the different communities. Eyes teared, and voices choked. After fifteen years, the land legalization process had come to a close. Each of Valle Nuevo's *campesino* families would have, in the eyes of the world, official ownership of the lots they farm and that sit underneath their homes! Those who for generations were treated as indentured servants, had arrived at land security. The scale of this transfer to achieve land reform for this many *campesinos*, former refugees who had been systemically dispossessed, was beyond anything that had happened in El Salvador. It was a matter of moving heaven and earth, not just for Valle Nuevo, SMC, and partners, but also for the Salvadoran government and its agencies.

The legalization story was long and winding, filled with twists and turns, bureaucratic roadblocks, unforeseen fees and costs, changes in laws and agencies, and entirely new administrations. The elders of the *directiva* served longer than their respective terms and beyond their personal desire in order to see the project through. The *campesinos* held numerous fundraisers, and the brothers and sisters of SMC and other friends of Valle Nuevo reached in their pockets not just once or twice but many times to find the necessary funds for yet a new requirement.

Along the way we did discover, however, many new friends who would help, allies who were creative, flexible, and resourceful, and partners who prayed and made financial donations. Just as Margarita recognized signs of God's faithfulness in the light on the path when the community was fleeing to Honduras and then in the rainbow in front of them when they returned, we saw in the contributions of so many the *acompañamiento* of the Lord. God's desire was to bring us into the promised land.

And God is still leading us. The improbability of this now twenty-five-year-old transnational relationship is evidence—at least to us—that the divine is at play. We are just ordinary people. We understand very well that it is not natural for the *campesinos* to vulnerably open themselves to outside people who have been part of the world that has oppressed them. It is challenging for them to turn their homes, moreover their bedrooms, over to those who cannot understand them. It is uncommon for those from the states to return to the same place year-after-year, now decade-after-decade, spending limited travel money and occasionally sacrificing health. It can produce anxiety for the first-timers to travel not for the purpose of tourism but for a relationship with people who live so differently and speak another language.

In May, 2016, Morena reported on the *directiva's* review of chapters five and six of this book, "We realized we are defying the chasm; we know this because we truly feel very close to you." The chasm and the transnational communion are contemporaries, but not for long. Our common story can now be measured in decades, and the relationship is being passed on to new generations. Some guilt has been assuaged, and some self-esteem has been gained. We interpret these signs to mean that this communion can defy and fill and thereby erase the chasm.

There is a requirement of us, however: perseverance. Any important relationship requires intentionality, self-sacrifice, and discipline. For us this challenge is exacerbated by the historical, political, social, and spiritual reality of the chasm that lies between us. We are separated by three international borders, mountain ranges, expensive travel, language, and culture. Without conscious effort our relationship will evaporate.

Defying the chasm means we must continue practicing our five practices: never denying the power of suffering, giving thanks in all that we do, sharing whatever we have, remembering our history, and proclaiming the death of Christ until he comes again. We must also remember the four lessons we have learned: no matter the circumstances or setbacks, we will celebrate, we will accompany each other in all things, we will consider our possessions as communal property, and we will call each other to courage.

All of our communities are highly relational, and they continue to exist because we have developed over the years skills that we practice every day in our local scene. These same relational skills need to be developed for inter-community relationships to grow.

On a daily basis we need to be attentive and conscious that life is happening three countries away either to the south or the north. Our brothers and sisters in places that seem remote to us are having birthdays, anniversaries, accidents, and illnesses. They are commemorating special events in their own community's history. A photograph of others placed strategically

Section 3: The Table of Creation

in our homes or a date noted on our calendars can remind us with whom we are now family. In the body of Christ we laugh, celebrate, cry, and grieve with each other. We should be able to do the same for those who are far away as well as for those who are close by.

Mindfulness of each other as a daily discipline prepares our spirits so that our less frequent opportunities for direct communication will be fruitful and rich. Face-to-face visits are by far the best way we can build relationships, but we need to supplement these with the communication opportunities that technology can provide us through email, Skype, FaceBook, and other social media. Phone calls don't have to be lengthy to communicate that we are thinking of each other. Electronic communication can be frustrating when internet signals are lost or there hasn't been money to purchase more minutes on a Salvadoran cellphone. Nevertheless, persistence brings rewards, and a simple thing like a monthly date to call a family or friend in the north or the south can help close the chasm.

Nothing can match the power of an in-person conversation or of telling stories or planning projects while sitting in a circle. Since it does not appear visits from south to north will become politically more feasible anytime soon, the annual delegation trips increase in their importance. Having a number of SMC members make their first visit to Valle Nuevo as well as having others return for their second and third or fifth and tenth visits are equally high priorities.

Visits also help add to our storehouse of stories. There are the annual events that are part of every delegation such as the hike to the Lempa and the meal that follows in Sensuntepeque. We have enjoyed workshops on many topics with activities that make us laugh, dream, and reflect together. We have discussed with each other, compared notes, and given counsel on the challenges of living in community, of preparing younger leadership, and of dealing with internal and external politics. In addition to these collective and often planned encounters, there are the regular happenings of life that friends always share with friends: births, marriages, deaths, and detentions by immigration officials.

Telling and retelling stories, new as well as old, helps build our identity and sense of community. Those from SMC have listened to the *campesinos'* story of fleeing across the Lempa River many times. Now, that story is shared with the children and youth in the communities in the north. They too, can tell the story, even if they have never visited Valle Nuevo. Storytelling is not difficult; it comes naturally for almost all of us. And most are good as well at listening to the stories of others. For those few of us who struggle in the telling or the listening, we need to recognize stories are a gift given for the welfare of the whole.

In a Hope Fellowship homily about God's reconciliation with people, Matt Porter stated, "When it comes to atonement, stories are literally all that we have." This is true also of our reconciliation or at-one-ment with each other. Our unity is not achieved through the application of abstract principles, the affirmation of a set of values, or the practice of laudable virtues; instead it is discovered in the interpretation of our history. In our stories is the pronouncement of forgiveness and the declaration of healing.

This tendency to interpret our experience theologically should be encouraged. The elders' experience in Valle Nuevo of the base community movement prior to the civil war has taught us all the importance of engaging the biblical narrative in order to find our place in our world today. We should continue our practice of gathering in every delegation, both on a Valle Nuevo verandah as well as in the meeting with SMC delegates and university students in the Torogóz salon, for theological reflection with the stories of Scripture, of *Monseñor* Romero, and of our own experiences. Whenever we read and discern collectively, we are enriched, encouraged, and challenged. Every time we turn to God's word, we become more aware that together we are God's people, and the "we" and "they" distinction fades in our consciousness.

All of this emphasis on communication, of course, highlights the deficiency that some feel in their language skills in either Spanish or English. When we are together our shared language of tears, hugs, smiles, washing each other's feet, and gentle gestures such as a hand placed upon another's hand, can transcend the limitation of words. Nevertheless, more of us need to commit or recommit ourselves to learning a few basic phrases in the other language and then gather our courage to try them out.

In order to persevere in all of these wonderful things, we must look beyond our immediate circumstances and see with eyes of faith. Good intentions alone will not deliver us for there are many things—our desire for instant gratification, our discouragement when our efforts don't produce immediate results, our inclination to spend time only with those who are like us—keep us from knowing God's deeper truth and the fullness of God's joy.

We can turn to Scripture to find inspiration from those who have been faithful. Moses came before Pharaoh multiple times to ask for the release of the Hebrew people. Daniel in exile stayed true to his identity as a person of God even when he was given opportunities to accommodate and make

SECTION 3: THE TABLE OF CREATION

his own life easier. Hannah, Samuel's mother-to-be, pled and prayed for a child again and again. Jesus told the story of the unjust judge who would not deny the persistent widow; a group of companions boldly overcame the obstacles of a crowd, heights, and a roof to place their paralytic friend before Jesus for healing; and the woman with the issue of blood pushed pass a multitude in order to touch Jesus. And we have our own stories that can remind us of God's faithfulness, such as the fifteen-year journey to land legalization. More than once we fattened turkeys for a celebration only to discover new government hurdles. December 20, 2016, however, finally came, and land titles were received.

Our stories also consistently acknowledge and affirm that this relationship is a gift, and it is this realization more than anything else that can give us the strength to do the hard work of building and nurturing our relationship with each other.

We walk into the future, remembering our past, living into our present, and discerning together our next steps. We will admit, though, the future can look daunting for all of our communities. For starters, recent tests have shown that Valle Nuevo and Santa Marta have a serious problem with their drinking water. A system that was built more than fifteen years ago is in need of expensive repairs so that it can once again provide potable water. Meanwhile gang violence in El Salvador continues to take a heavy toll on the youth of the community, many of whom, fearing for their lives, have fled to find safety. Changes in the political climate of the United States have left us with concerns that travel from south to north or visits back to El Salvador from those who have already immigrated may become more difficult than ever.

Several of the SMC communities have struggled with shortages of leadership, identity issues, and other conflicts, in some cases due to the deaths or other transitions of founders and leaders. In early 2017, Plow Creek Fellowship decided after much work and counsel with other communities, that it would need to disband. Discerning how to follow God's will and bear witness to the love of Jesus Christ in a society with rapidly changing mores and values while navigating generational shifts in how communication takes place and how community is experienced can be overwhelming.

We could be tempted to focus solely on our local community and on our own problems, but our salvation is found in defying the chasm. Our sorrow has been divided and parceled as we've shared it with one another across the divide. Our joy increases as we engage God's goodness north and south. Our relationship with each other has informed and impacted all of our communities. For example, patterns of growth established in the base communities of Latin America influenced Hope Fellowship's response to increasing numbers when it chose a few years ago to worship in smaller clusters that could meet in homes rather than building or renting a larger space.

We have been enriched by common exploration of the Scriptures, each coming from our own cultural and historical vantage points. Because of this relationship, God's presence in our souls has become more prominent and our view of the world has grown in our spirits.

Morena's faithfulness in her calling provides a picture of the future for all of us as we continue this journey of friendship. She earned her master's degree in early childhood education and returned to Valle Nuevo to pursue her vocation of preparing youngsters to be the next generation of community leaders. Even after waiting several years, she was not able to get a government-funded teaching position in the Santa Marta school, but she knew that the children are the future of Valle Nuevo and Santa Marta.

With the help of her colleagues, Teresa de Jesús Escalante and Maribel Ascensio, and a group of parents that live some distance from the community school in the village center, she searched for a location that could house a small class for preschoolers, what in the United States would be the equivalent of Head Start. After a year she received permission from a small school operating in a two-room house to use its second room. She then proceeded to create the educational materials that would be needed and find the practical equipment such as mattresses for the children's rest time. With the help of the parents, the school was launched in 2016. The SMC delegation in June of that year enjoyed spending time with the young children of the class and were inspired by the fruit of Morena's vision.

With the school up and running, Morena, Teresa, and Maribel appealed to the mayor of the municipality of Victoria for help in locating a new space since the class would soon be displaced by the computer lab of the small school co-housed in the same building. She had to make multiple trips to the city just to get the mayor's attention. Many new requirements surfaced, but after several months she was authorized to use an abandoned building with no roof or door and walls and floors covered with graffiti.

Transforming the structure to become a center for learning was daunting. The teachers, the parents of the children, and Morena's family lobbied the mayor and persuaded him to put on a roof, install a door, and donate

Section 3: The Table of Creation

paint to cover the walls of the large room. The parents are currently working on building a small outdoor kitchen and latrine. With funds from SMC the group was able to fence the property, providing safety for the children and space for a future garden.

This longed-for future garden is a metaphor for our communities as we lean into the future. The work of gardening—the tilling and preparation of the land for planting, the scattering of seeds, the watering and weeding of unwelcomed growth—will itself help form and develop the young ones in the early childhood school. And then its produce will satisfy their hunger and help them grow strong. As it is with tomatoes, so it is with our transnational relationship. The work of caring for it, as well as the sustenance it provides, will help us grow and pass life on to future generations.

As we celebrate twenty-five years of this relationship, it is natural to look ahead and wonder if we will be celebrating together in another twenty-five. Can we say with confidence we have learned the right lessons, earned the wisdom, and so discerned the desire of God that in 2042 our communities will likely be visiting each other, calling each other, and holding each other in our hearts? No. We can say that with assurance.

We do not know what will have transpired in global markets and politics that will affect our nation states and the ability to travel one direction or the other. We do not know if border walls will still be unassailable and if the economic divide still sharply drawn. These things are unknowable.

If we wanted to simply preserve this relationship for the future, we would have institutionalized it. But communion is the living breath of the Holy Spirit. Institutionalized communion is ultimately not communion at all. This is the reason that communities and their relationships come and go. So far God has given the perfect gifts for the given day and the current need. We will seek to pass along to the next generation passion for building *shalom*, a vision of the table of creation, and a hunger for justice. Then we will wait to see what God provides for tomorrow.

To those friends who are reading and are not part of Valle Nuevo or Shalom Missions, we stress again, our story is both unique and universal. Unique only in that it is our story, filled with our names and our circumstances. Universal in that it is just one more story of the adventure and blessing of God's grace coming to those who seek healing and forgiveness. It is a gift from heaven, but not one that simply fell into our lap. Yvonne Dilling, on behalf of the people of Valle Nuevo, was looking for someone who would accompany them. David Janzen, on behalf of the people of Shalom

Mission Communities, was seeking a way to stand in solidarity with those who had been victimized by the war that the United States had helped initiate and finance. Their long walk and conversation planted a seed that they and others tended and nurtured.

For those of us in Valle Nuevo and SMC, let's remember that each conversation, every visit, all of our phone calls and Facebook posts, each delegation visit, every hike to the Lempa, and all of our shared meals defy the chasm. Our prayer is that one day in the fullness of time, not just the gate, but also the wall itself will be torn down and we will live together in a community of *shalom* where there is plenty for all rather than extravagance for some.

Lazarus, the man who was formerly known as poor will no longer be poor. The man who was formerly known as rich will no longer be rich, but he will have a name. Privilege will give way to mutuality. Death to the chasm! During the day we will sing at our labors, and in the evening we will sit down to eat with glad and generous hearts at the table of creation. We will know that we are joined together in Christ.

Amen.

Discussion Guide for Those from the North

IN PREPARATION FOR DISCUSSION

1. How have mission trips shaped your faith and worldview?
2. What are the mission goals or objectives of your church or community?

INTRODUCTION

1. What is your initial reaction to the authors' suggestion that U.S. mission efforts have been influenced by imperialism and/or American exceptionalism?
2. What is your experience and understanding of communion? Does the description of "transnational communion" (pages 11–14) resonate with you?
3. On one side of the chasm are those of the United States who have economic privilege and were complicit in the Salvadoran war. On the other are the *campesinos,* victims of generations of colonialism and a war in which they were chased from their homes. Is this a legitimate context for interpreting the parable of the great chasm? What are the respective needs in this relationship of these two groups?
4. In the *Vamos Todos* hymn (pages 15–16), what do you think the stanza "everyone has a place and a mission to share" means in the context of an international Christian relationship?

DISCUSSION GUIDE FOR THOSE FROM THE NORTH

CHAPTER 1—THE WITNESS OF ROMERO

1. Why does Latin American consider Romero a patron saint?
2. Who are the transformative, Romero-like figures in the United States? What are the differences?
3. How does *Monseñor* Romero's story help you understand the Kingdom of God?

CHAPTER 2—BEGINNING OF A FRIENDSHIP

1. What sets friendships apart from other kinds of relationships?
2. What would "mission trips" look like that are centered on friendship over time?

CHAPTER 3—SUFFERING

1. How is suffering described and embraced in your faith community?
2. Why are the ethics (doing) and the ecclesiology (community) of suffering more challenging to accept in the United States than for faith communities in developing countries?
3. How can suffering help bridge differences, fears, or insecurities that hinder transnational or transcultural relationships?

CHAPTER 4—GIVING THANKS

1. Please re-read the story of Margarita and her altar on page 59. What "altars" do you have in place personally or within your faith community that remind you of God's faithfulness?
2. "We have all of the tortillas we can eat, this is what makes us thankful... this is the promised land." Is thanks-giving itself theological reflection? Why or why not?

Discussion Guide for Those from the North

CHAPTER 5—SHARING

1. How is the kind of sharing described in this chapter different from traditional Christian mission relationships? How is it similar?
2. Do you believe the kind of sharing through *acompañamiento* (accompanying one another through hardships) is spiritually possible between two faith communities divided by physical distance and boundaries (page 73)? If so, how?
3. Can you describe a time you experienced *acompañamiento*? How did this experience of walking alongside another change you?
4. What are the pitfalls of economic sharing or development work sponsored by a more affluent community on behalf of a community "outside the gate?" What are your thoughts on SMC's reluctance to provide help and its eventual decision to do so?

CHAPTER 6—REMEMBERING

1. How is the act of remembering spiritual, social, and political (page 94)?
2. In what ways can the act of remembering serve as an "assault on the hostility of a border (page 94)? How are borders hostile? How are they beneficial?
3. Why is remembering so difficult? What are the ways you have found in long-term relationships to remember and acknowledge important occasions in the lives of others who are far away?

CHAPTER 7—PROCLAIMING

1. What role does Christ play in uniting two faith communities divided by social, socioeconomic, political, and spiritual chasms?
2. Do the authors come down on one side in the classic debate between "being faithful" and "being responsible for results?" For what are we ultimately held accountable by God?

CHAPTER 8—LESSONS LEARNED

1. How might the new individual land titles for the 171 families in Valle Nuevo impact the communal practice and ethic of Valle Nuevo and Shalom Mission communities?
2. Can the ongoing costs of yearly delegation visits (south to north or north to south) be justified? If so, why? Would it be better if money was simply sent to Valle Nuevo?
3. Of the following principles expressed in this chapter (celebration, companionship, community, and courage) which one most resonates with you? Why?

CHAPTER 9—
LOOKING FORWARD: OUR CALL TO ACTION

1. How, if at all, has your understanding of traditional mission relationships been challenged by the practices of transnational communion?
2. Is "transnational communion" a viable vision for uniting faith communities divided by chasms?
3. How and why is a transnational relationship a gift?

WRAP-UP

Compose a couple of questions based on this book that would be suitable for a *campesino* community that has read or listened to *Compañeros y Compañeras*.

Bibliography

Dilling, Yvonne. *In Search of Refuge.* Harrisonburg, VA: Harold Press, 1984.
Janzen, David. *The Intentional Christian Community Handbook: For Idealists, Hypocrites, and Wannabe Disciples of Jesus.* Brewster, MA: Paraclete, 2012.
Miles, Ann. *From Cuenca to Queens: An Anthropological Story of Transnational Migration.* Austin: University of Texas Press, 2004.
Perla, Hector. "Monsenor Romero's Resurrection: Transnational Salvadoran Organizing." *NACLA Report* (Nov/Dec 2010) 25–30.